BIL WRIGHT

Putting Makeup
on the Fat Boy

CORNELSEN
ENGLISH
LIBRARY

Cornelsen

CORNELSEN **ENGLISH** LIBRARY
Bil Wright · Putting Makeup on the Fat Boy

Verlagsredaktion
Michael Dunkel

Umschlaggestaltung
hawemannundmosch, Konzeption und Gestaltung, Berlin

Titelbild
Corbis, Düsseldorf (oben (M): A. Chederros/Onoky, unten (M): Pete Starman)

Gestaltung & technische Umsetzung
Buchgestaltung + Berlin

Passende Arbeitsblätter und weitere Hilfen zu diesem Titel gibt es unter:
www.cornelsen.de/cel

www.cornelsen.de

1. Auflage, 2. Druck 2024
Alle Drucke dieser Auflage sind inhaltlich unverändert und können
im Unterricht nebeneinander verwendet werden.

Druck: H. Heenemann, Berlin

ISBN 978-3-06-033821-4

PEFC zertifiziert
Dieses Produkt stammt aus nachhaltig
bewirtschafteten Wäldern und kontrollierten
Quellen.

PEFC
PEFC/04-31-1156

www.pefc.de

CONTENTS

When I was twelve, I convinced my mother to let me do her makeup for Parents' Night. When I was finished, my sister, Rosalia, who was fifteen, said, "Ma, aren't ya even gonna say anything?"

5 Ma said to me, "All right, so it looks nice, Carlos. But I don't think I should be encouraging something like this. I'm not gonna go to your school and tell your teacher, 'See my face! Isn't it pretty? My son did my makeup. Didn't he do an excellent job?'"

10 Rosalia asked, "Why not?"

Ma said, "You know why not! Don't make me say it."

Rosalia put her hands on her hips. "You know what, Ma? Carlos is *talented*, that's what he is. He's probably gonna be famous one day for being so talented, and you 15 should be happy he can do something this good so young!"

After Ma went to Parents' Night, Rosalia and I went to McDonald's. Rosalia told me again she thought I was talented and that I was gonna be famous. I asked her to buy me an extra bag of chocolate chip cookies and an all-20 chocolate sundae to prove she really meant it.

. . .

By the time I got to Sojourner Truth/John F. Kennedy Freedom High School, I knew if other people could get paid as makeup artists, I could too. I already had a job after school being an assistant to all the teachers in a day care 25 program. I didn't love my job, but I did love being able to go shopping for makeup at Little Ricky's on Thirteenth

Street, where they had the wildest stuff. I'd run home, lock my bedroom door, and try it out immediately. Sitting on the side of my bed, studying my face in my two-sided makeup mirror (one for normal view, one for super-close-up) was like school after school. It was me practicing the thing that I knew would make me famous someday.

No matter what any of them said, the girls at school had to admit I was an expert. And the boys who got away with eyeliner because they were supposedly rockers even asked me for tips on how to put it on straight. I was really happy to tell them, because crooked eyeliner is so whack, it makes me nuts.

My friend Angie suggested, "Carlos, now that you're sixteen, you should come to Macy's and try to get a part-time job at a makeup counter." She worked there on Saturdays and she bugged me from the beginning of school in September. "You have to go and apply for a job before the holidays. That's when they need all the help they can get. I bet you could work for any company you wanted— Chanel, Bobbi Brown, Dolce & Gabbana. Any of them."

I know it sounds like I'm exaggerating, but the idea of it made me stop breathing for… well, a few seconds at least. I don't know why I hadn't thought of it first. I guess I'd only pictured doing Mary J. Blige's makeup before a concert, or going on tour with Rihanna because she insisted if she didn't have me she couldn't do the tour. I hadn't thought about working at a department store.

"Angie, do you think a famous store like Macy's would really hire me? I don't have any professional experience."

And good old Angie said, "Honey, all we have to do is get you an application. Then we'll come up with a fake résumé. We'll put my cell number on it. When they call,

I'll answer, 'Greenberg's Department Store' and tell them, 'Carlos Duarte? You'd be lucky to get him! He's fabulous!'"

Angie worked on the tenth floor in the Linens department at Macy's. But selling pillowcases and Martha Stewart sheet sets didn't mean she knew a whole lot about how they hired people in the makeup department. "I'm pretty sure it's not that easy, Angie. Can't you make friends with somebody at one of the counters and ask them how they hire?"

And of course Angie said, "I can't go down there! They all look so beautiful... and so *mean*."

"Are you kidding me? 'They all look so beautiful'? I've passed by makeup counters hundreds of times, including the ones at Macy's, and the people who work at those counters have on a ton of makeup, but that doesn't mean they're beautiful! And if they look mean, maybe it's because it's hot standing around under those fluorescent lights wearing that much makeup whether you want to or not. Can you just get over yourself and go down and ask them? Get me a stupid application? This is important!"

"Maybe if I lose five pounds by Saturday when I go to work, I'll get up the courage to ask one of them."

"But, Angie, they don't care how much you weigh! And I guarantee you, you have a prettier face than most of them. Look, if you want, I'll get up early on Saturday and come over to your apartment and do your makeup."

"All right! If you do my makeup, I'll go down to the first floor on my break and ask one of those mean, snotty-looking would-be models how to apply for a job there. Making it absolutely clear that I don't mean for myself! And I'll do it whether I've lost five pounds or not."

"Ooooh!" I squealed, and yes, I do definitely squeal, I have to admit it. And the more excited I am, the higher it is. "Do you promise?"

"Yessssss, I promise!" Angie rolled her eyes and shook
5 her head. Then she said, "If you promise *me* something!"

"Anything, Ange, anything!" I knew she was gonna ask that, when we both worked at Macy's, I do her makeup every Saturday, and I was more than happy to say yes.

She looked at me very seriously and said, "You better
10 promise that when you get hired there and everybody knows you and thinks you're talented and great..."

"And they will," I flicked my head to the side with one hand on my hip. "You know they will, girl."

"Yeah, well you better promise that no matter how
15 popular you are, you won't start acting weird like you're embarrassed to be with me or something."

"Angie," I said, just as serious as she was, "I'm sorry you have this condition that makes you say and even think insane things. So, what I'm going to do until you can get
20 yourself healed is just say, hon, I love you and I'll always love you, whether you're a hundred and three pounds or three hundred and one pounds. I'm just hoping that you won't wind up being three hundred and one pounds."

Angie said, "And I don't think we have to worry about
25 me ever being a hundred and three pounds, unless somebody sews my mouth shut!" She laughed, one of her big old Angie laughs, which is one of my favorite sights and sounds in the world.

And I started picturing myself behind the biggest, most
30 fabulous makeup counter in Macy's.

CHAPTER 2

I went to Burrito Take-Out Village to tell my sister, Rosalia, that I was going to be working at Macy's very soon, and I'd share my discount with her. I couldn't believe she was going to school to be a medical technician at a place she'd
5 learned about from a poster on the subway. She was calling it college and working at Burrito Take-Out Village to pay for it. Okay, so getting such crummy grades that she couldn't go to a real college was no one's fault but her own. It was just that all we'd ever talked about, sitting on
10 the side of her bed while she let me try out different combinations of eye shadow on her, was how we were not gonna end up like our mother, managing a dry cleaner's and not being able to afford anything unless it was on sale.

"I saw the cutest jacket," Ma would say. "I'm gonna
15 keep checking back. Eventually they'll put it on sale." Or the worst was, "My boss says if somebody doesn't claim this coat in the next few weeks, he's gonna let me have it. Isn't that great!" Ugh. And we'd have to say, yeah, it was great, because neither one of us could afford to buy her a
20 winter coat, so better an unclaimed one from the cleaner's she worked in than no winter coat at all.

Rosalia said she used to think maybe our father would show up out of nowhere and we'd live happily ever after, but then she realized she'd been watching too many soap
25 operas. She said she kind of remembered him from when she was little, but the only details were that he was "tall and had red eyes."

"Tall with red eyes, Rosalia? That sounds like the devil."

Rosalia laughed. "Yeah, that's pretty much how Ma describes him too." According to Ma, he left when Rosalia was five and I was two. When we do bring him up, which is hardly at all these days, Ma makes this face as though she smells dog crap somewhere in the room. "If we have to talk about the drunken drug addict, I'm leaving the room," she says. And Rosalia and I look at each other and laugh. It's like a joke now, our father the joke, the smell in the room. Was he really a drunken drug addict? When I asked Ma, she said, "What? You think I'd tell my kids their father was a drunken drug addict if it wasn't true?"

Ma hates all the boys she's ever seen Rosalia with, and says, "If you think you're gonna bring another bum in here for me to cook for, you're nuts." Now Rosalia's going out with this cook at Burrito Take-Out Village named Danny, so she came home and said to Ma, "This one's not a bum, Ma. And he can cook dinner for *you*. So don't start in on him."

I can't believe my sister really wants to spend the rest of her life looking at other people's X-rays. And now she's talking about getting engaged to Danny, who I have not-so-great feelings about. Maybe it's because he's never once looked me right in the eye, and because every time I go into Burrito Take-Out Village, all the other guys in the kitchen say stuff in Spanish that I don't understand, and then they laugh, and Danny doesn't exactly laugh, but he *does* snicker. If Rosalia understands, she pretends she doesn't, except once she whipped her head around and said, "Screw you. You think I'm deaf?"

But the news about Macy's was too good to wait, even though it hadn't happened yet. So I decided to go first to Rosalia at Burrito Take-Out Village and tell her and then decide how much to tell my ma, since I knew she wouldn't be all that crazy about the makeup part.

When I got to Rosalia's job, she was busy taking orders, so I had to wait. Danny saw me come in. As usual, he didn't say hi or anything. He just kept cooking. But when his buddy whistled and said something stupid in Spanish, Danny grinned. Rosalia must have been too busy to hear, or else she was ignoring it. When she finally had a second, I went up to the counter and said as quickly as I could, "Guess what! Angie's gonna find out how I can get a job at Macy's doing makeup on the weekends, and after they hire me, I promise to let you use my discount. Won't it be *beyond crazy fabulous*!"

I could see out of the corner of my eye Danny at the grill behind Rosalia looking at me. All right, I'm not stupid. It was raining hard and my mascara may have been smudged a little from so much rain.

Rosalia didn't have time to say a whole lot. She told me in this low voice, "Carlos, your eyes are all smeary. We can talk when I get home." So I left. On the way home I decided not to tell my mother at all until I was hired.

CHAPTER 3

The next Saturday, I got up early and went from East Fifth Street, where we lived, up to Sixteenth, where Angie lived. Her mother stared at me all over and said, "I've heard a lot about you. As close as Angie says you two are, I'm surprised I haven't met you before."

I said, "Well... I'm here now," and tried to make it sound intelligent even though I felt stupid as soon as I'd said it. I hadn't met her because Angie had admitted that her mother would think I was weird. So why would I volunteer to go to her house to have one more person think I was weird?

"She's back there." Angie's mother pointed, still doing her survey of me.

As I passed her parents' bedroom on the way to Angie's bedroom, her father came out in an ugly green uniform and called out, "Why's he going into Angie's room?"

Angie's mother said loudly from the kitchen, "I told you before, he's going to do her makeup." And her father said, "I still don't know what the hell that means! But whatever it means, he can do it out here!"

I was caught in the hallway, facing his big belly. I turned right around, heading for the living room, wishing Angie would come out of her stupid bedroom already. I sat on the couch with my Vuitton Neverfull bag on my lap, trying to pretend I didn't know he was still there, observing me like I was an exotic insect. (And no, I don't have a real Vuitton, but it's the best imitation *I've* ever seen).

Finally, when Angie's father did go into the kitchen, there was all this whispering. It wasn't hard to figure out that he thought the circus had come to town, and Angie's mother was saying it was fine, it would be gone soon.

As soon as Angie came out, I knew we were in trouble. "If I do your makeup," I said as quietly as I could, "you can't wear that."

"What do you mean, I can't wear this!" she started whining immediately. "I love polka dots! Polka dots are my favorite. That's why I'm wearing them today. To give me courage."

"First of all, polka dots are your favorite because you're a psycho. And I don't really care if you wear them any other day but today. Today I'm doing a smoky eye for daytime in shades of gray and you should wear something subtle, like—"

"I know. You want me to wear black like those vampires at the makeup counters. And that's what *you* get to do after they hire you. But I don't wanna wear all black. It makes me depressed. And I have to work eight hours, telling people the difference between a king-size bed and a twin—believe it or not—so I can't afford to be depressed. I want my polka dots!"

"Then, fine!" I knew there wasn't time to try to convince her, and I certainly didn't want her parents to come rushing in from the other room to defend her. I knew her father would be only too happy to throw me out. I reached into my bag and pulled out my makeup case. "I'll work *around* the polka dots!"

About thirty minutes later, in spite of the polka dots, Angie had a daytime look to rock all of Macy's and to definitely impress the makeup counter divas. Even she was impressed, and I'd done her makeup dozens of times. "Should I tell them you did it?" she asked me.

"That's the point, Angie girl, that's the point! That, and an application!"

She called me on her morning break to say that she was too nervous to go downstairs to the makeup counters, and I tried really hard not to say anything mean enough to hurt our friendship. But I was furious. If she was that nervous, who knew if she'd ever have the guts to go down and ask *anything?*

"Angie, I won't hate you if you don't go talk to those people. I'll just be very disappointed."

5 There was silence on the other end. All she said was, "I'm really sorry, honey."

But at twelve thirty Miss Beyoncé Knowles's "Irreplaceable" started ringing in my jeans and I hoped for a miracle.

"Hi, Miss Angie Girl," I said gently. What I heard on the
10 other end was a shriek.

"I did it, I did it, I did it!"

I looked up at the ceiling and said, "Thank you, God!"

"The thing is," Angie said, somehow already back to her familiar whine, "it's not as easy as we thought, Carlos! It's
15 really hard!"

"What's really hard?" I wanted her to be clear and specific and encouraging.

She repeated, "It's a lot, Carlos! Really a lot! It's not as easy as we thought at all!"

20 I refused to get psyched-out without knowing the details. What was a lot for Angie didn't have to be the same from my point of view. "I didn't think it would be easy, Angie. I didn't think it would be anything, because I didn't have any information! So, what is the information
25 you have that makes you think it will be so hard?"

"I can't tell you now. It would take too long. I'll tell you when I get home."

"Angie, please! I've waited all morning for this. Can't you tell me *anything*?"

30 "No, Carlos, no! My lunchtime is almost over and I haven't had anything to eat." Well, I didn't know how that could be true, since she'd been talking with her mouth full

14

both times she'd been on the phone. But I knew if it was a choice between me and food, I didn't have a prayer. "All right." I gave her a big sigh, "I'll wait. But can you at least tell me what counter you went to, to ask."

5 Angie started giggling. I knew it had to be something incredible. "Well? You can't do this, Miss Angie! Spill it!"

"FEEEAATTTUURRE FAACCCEE!" she screamed into the phone.

I smiled. *Well! You go, Angie! If we're gonna shoot for it, let's* 10 *shoot for the top!* "Angie, you know how much I love you, don't you? Even though sometimes I think somebody is paying you to make me legally insane, I do love you. And I will wait until you get home tonight to tell me what the people at the FeatureFace counter said about how fast I'll 15 become famous working for them."

"Oooo, Carlos, I'm just warning you. It will not be easy!"

I had enough positive information now that I didn't have to even consider anything else. "Do I need an 20 application, Angie?"

"Yes."

"And do you have one for me?"

"Yes. I had to be superpersistent, because nobody at that counter was paying any attention to anyone except— 25 are you ready for this? Shirlena Day! "

"Shirlena Day! Was she there?"

"Yep, and everyone was running in circles trying to get all the stuff she was asking for. It was crazy, crazy! But I did manage to get you an application."

30 "Darling, that's all Carlos has to know."

When I shut my phone, I was already trying to figure out once I was working weekends, how long would it take before FeatureFace begged me to quit school to work for them full-time? Then I thought about Shirlena Day being a customer. I'd watched her on *Smokin' Friday Nights* a few times and I thought she was a comedic genius. As a matter of fact, I thought she was the funniest person on the show. Why wasn't I working for FeatureFace right now? By next month I'd be right in the middle of a *Vogue* spread with Shirlena Day quoted as saying, "I discovered Carlos Duarte working behind the FeatureFace counter at Macy's, and I haven't been able to live without him since!"

I could make it happen. I knew I could. But first... FeatureFace had to hire me!

CHAPTER 4

We met at the Dunkin' Donuts halfway between Angie's house and mine. I insisted we sit at a back booth so Angie wouldn't get distracted, which she did quite easily. Especially if it was a boy with dark hair, who looked like he'd lifted any kind of weights at all. All Angie had to see was some evidence of pecs and the dark hair and it was over! She'd order another hot chocolate, two more chocolate-covered donuts, and stare. You could get up, go shopping, get your hair cut, and come back, and if the guy was still there, Angie would not have noticed you weren't. Luckily, when Angie met me to discuss Macy's and FeatureFace, there were only screaming kids and their mothers in there.

Angie hugged me, "I'm so excited, Carlos! They thought my makeup was fabulous, and they can't wait for you to come in."

"Is that true?" By the time I saw Angie, her makeup
5 was a total mess and I would have told anybody who asked that I'd had nothing to do with it.

She reached into her bag and pulled out the application, but before I could even look at the application, her face changed completely. It was the now-I-have-something-
10 too-tragic-to-tell-you face. "The thing is, Carlos, while I was there, there was this other poor girl there who was being interviewed. They were barely paying her any attention because Shirlena Day was there. But I saw how they do it." Angie shook her head like we were suddenly
15 in a funeral home staring down at a coffin, with my chances of ever working for FeatureFace in it.

"This girl had her résumé there, and the counter manager was looking at it and saying mean things about it."

20 "Whadya mean, 'mean things'?"

"Oh, you know, like 'I've never heard of this place' or 'They didn't keep you there very long, did they?' It was awful. I felt so sorry for the girl. Then a salesperson would ask for something that Shirlena Day wanted, and he'd
25 snap at them like they were idiots."

"Was Shirlena nice or was she a creep?" I asked Angie.

"No," Angie said, "she seemed pretty nice. She kept telling them, 'I can have my assistant phone in an order,' but they wanted to seal the deal on the spot. So every time
30 she mentioned something she liked that FeatureFace made, they went crazy, bringing out cases and cases of it."

"I can't stand it, Ange," I squealed. "I wish I'd been there. I wish I could've been working for them already!"

"I'm tellin ya'," Angie said, slurping hot chocolate, "ya gotta get the job first, ya gotta get past this dude Valentino. And he's like a guard dog." Her mouth was so covered with sugar, she looked like she was wearing frosted lipstick. "Because the counter was so hysterical, I had to wait forever before I could even speak to him. After he finished insulting the girl's résumé, he said, 'I don't suppose you have a portfolio, do you?' And I thought, She's toast now, burnt freakin' toast! But she had this book of pictures of the makeup she'd done. I didn't see the pictures, but all I kept thinking was you probably don't have any pictures like that, do you?"

"No... ," I said, annoyed both that Angie was so sure of what I didn't have and also that she was right.

"Then, she had this model with her. So after this Valentino guy looked at her book, he told her to go ahead and make up her model, which is when I got a chance to talk to him."

"So you said this guy really liked your makeup?"

"Yeah," Angie answered. "He liked it a lot. I mean, he didn't go on and on or anything. He just said, 'Your makeup is very well done.'"

"Then I'm gonna take your picture in the exact same makeup, and another one with a different outfit. And I'll get Rosalia to do the same thing. And Soraya, and Chantal at school. Maybe I won't have a lot of pictures, but the ones I have will be *beyond stunning*!"

Everybody deserves a chance, especially those who are as talented as I am, I thought. I made Angie sit right there at Dunkin'

18

Donuts and help me fill out the application. I knew I could get at least two of the guys who owned beauty salons in our neighborhood to say I'd worked as a makeup artist for them. Plus we added a couple of salons at the bottom of the list that we knew had gone out of business, so they couldn't be traced. The good part, I figured, was that I was young. How many places could I have worked?

The next week at school I did makeup on Chantal and Soraya and took pictures. I did a step-by-step with Chantal, which I thought was a genius idea, because it would show I really knew what I was doing and how I could change somebody's look completely. Chantal really got on my nerves during the photos and started asking how much she was getting paid, so I finally had to give her twenty-five dollars. But it taught me that when you ask somebody to do you a favor as your friend: (1) make sure they know what the word "favor" means, and (2) make sure they really are your friend. The reason I was hoping all the girls would not expect to get paid was because I was already paying this kid at school, Gleason Kraft, sixty dollars to take the pictures. So practically my whole paycheck from the day care center was used up.

Gleason Kraft was a rocker who was also in the photography club, and I knew he'd be great because I'd seen his photographs of concerts displayed around school. They looked like they were right out of magazines. He was in my homeroom, but the way I got to be friends with him was by telling him about products I knew he'd like for his rocker look. I told him that I knew a lot of rockers bought their makeup at Ricky's and there was one right near school. I also told him his hair was incredible when he dyed it jet black. He had this thick biracial hair thing going—you know, part curly, part fuzzy—and the way it looked with his gray eyes was insane! He looked a little embarrassed when I was going on and on like a twelve-year-old girl about his hair, but he also looked like he didn't mind the attention. If the world was perfect, I'd probably date Gleason Kraft, but only my dreams are perfect.

I told my girl Soraya, "I'm going to get a job at Macy's working for FeatureFace, and I have to do your makeup and take pictures of it."

Soraya is a manager at Tokyo Jo's on Eleventh St. It's a resale store where they sell top designer's clothes for a whole lot less. I don't get why exactly. As far as I can tell, there's not anything wrong with them. Even at the resale price, I can't usually afford them. When I told her I was getting the job, Soraya, who thinks managing Tokyo Jo's has made her Anna Wintour of *Vogue*, tried to correct me in her fake British accent. "You mean you have an interview, deah."

The truth was, I'd called the FeatureFace counter myself and they'd said yes, they were hiring, and someone would get back to me.

"No, I'm going to work for them, Soraya, just like I said. I just haven't told them yet."

That's when I think my girl got that we were making history. "Then you should do my pictures in the store," she said. "Give them makeup *and* haute couture!" Soraya put on a vintage Yves Saint Laurent, and we took mad pictures.

For Angie's shoot we went into a Catholic church that has prayer hours every day from twelve to one, so we went when we were on lunch. Angie thought it was weird, but that's because Angie doesn't have any sense of what a beauty shoot is. I've had subscriptions to *Vogue* and *Harper's Bazaar* since I was fourteen and could save up for them, so I knew that what I was doing was *beyond genius*. Gleason was going nuts shooting Angie in front of all the votive candles. For him it was photographer's heaven!

Finally it was time for Rosalia's pictures. I decided to take them in front of a bodega right across the street from Quik Clean & Press, the cleaner's my Ma managed. I wanted her to be proud of me, and one way of doing it was to let her look right across the street and see me telling a photographer how I wanted a picture of a model to look, and to have that model be her daughter.

That Friday I still hadn't heard whether FeatureFace even wanted to see me. But I knew I was going ahead with the shoot anyway. I'd convinced Rosalia not to say anything to Ma, so it would be a surprise.

Rosalia's version of family support that day was "You better make this good! And remember I gotta get to work, so don't take a lotta time!" I love my sister, but she has no idea about art or creativity. The point was, it was something Ma could be proud of, and Rosalia would be a part of it.

We went across the street to the bodega, and I knew Ma was in Quik Clean & Press, but I pretended I didn't even know the place existed. Angie was there as my assistant, and Gleason was in his pointy-toed boots and blue leather jacket, and people were stopping to watch us. I made Rosalia look pretty fierce, and even got her to let me put her hair back, which she hated, being the queen of superbig hair. I don't mean cool big like Gleason's. I mean, like, clown big. But I kept telling her, "Please, Rosalia, it's about the makeup. They can't see your makeup if they have to look through a hedge!" And she didn't love it, but she agreed to let me calm her hair down, way down.

We hadn't been there five minutes before my mother came out of the cleaner's. "Carlos! What are you doing?" she yelled across the street.

"It's a photo shoot, Ma! It's for FeatureFace Cosmetics! For Macy's!"

She stood there for a minute, with the cars going between us, her arms folded. Rosalia, of course, waved and yelled out, "Hi, Ma! I hate my hair!" So we lost a little of the professional atmosphere I was going for. But I could see that Ma was impressed.

. . .

"No, I haven't gotten the call yet, but I know it's coming and I have to be ready."

"Well, you're just a kid and they never heard of you, so don't get your hopes up," Ma told me at dinner. It was just her and me, since Rosalia was already at work.

A few mouthfuls later Ma asked me, "Do they even hire boys to do that at Macy's?"

"Ma," I said as patiently as I could, "you've been to Macy's. The whole first floor is full of men who are makeup artists."

"I never noticed," Ma said. She shrugged. "Well, like I said, you're a kid with no experience, so don't count on anything."

By the next Tuesday there was still no call from FeatureFace. I decided it meant God was giving me more time to get my act together. I thought about getting a book out of the library about how to interview for a job. I thought, *If I want to convince these people I'm going to be a star, I should interview like one.* So I watched talk shows like *Inside the Actors Studio*, where actors talked about how they got famous. I sat on my bed and leaned back to look relaxed, and smiled and talked out loud about how I knew that I was born to make people beautiful and how it was my personal campaign to stop people from acting ugly and they'd see how much better they looked.

When I did practice in the mirror, I was proud of myself. From the time I'd left junior high school, I'd looked like a different person. I'd given up potato chips, onion rings, french fries, fried rice, and donuts. Which also meant, at least in my mind, that I wasn't fat anymore, I was *big*. And *big* could mean anything—unlike "fat," which only meant one thing: FAT.

Even though by Wednesday morning there was still no call, I decided I only had two days to get my outfit together if I was going for my interview on Saturday. I went to Tokyo Jo's after school to see Soraya. Every once in a while she has something so marked down, she saves it for me, and sometimes it's so ugly that it's obvious why nobody else bought it. But sometimes it's truly a score nine and a half or a ten, and I can't resist it. I didn't really think I'd find anything for my interview that was in my budget, but I couldn't *not* look either.

"I think it's crazy to spend money when they haven't even called you yet," Soraya said before I could even close the store door behind me.

I tried on a pair of Cavalli pants that were too long and a little too tight, not to mention too expensive.

"You're such a shortie," she teased me. "You should go to a designer store for little kids."

"I would," I told her, "except I still wouldn't be able to afford anything."

My last try was an olive green turtleneck sweater by a company called Turtle that I'd never heard of. But that's exactly what I looked like in it, a turtle with hair, wearing a sweater. I should have known better. Maybe it's true that people with tan skin look good in olive green, but like with a lot of other things, I guess I'm the exception.

I was almost out of the store when I saw them, hanging from the ceiling in the corner, like someone was coming through from the roof feetfirst. All you could see were these thigh-high Stella McCartney boots. They were *beyond excellent.*

"Ohmygod! Soraya! They're beautiful!"

"I know," Soraya said like a cat that'd just had three cans of Friskies, as though she owned the Stella McCartneys herself.

"I want to try them on!"

"They're girls' boots, Carlos!"

"Duh! I still want to try them on!"

"They're also three hundred dollars, marked down from six hundred. They're not for playing dress-up with!"

"Soraya, there is nobody in here. It's not as though you're busy. Can you please get the boots down so I can try them on!"

"You are such a pain, Carlos! I don't know why I even put up with you!"

I just smiled at her, patiently, while she went to the back to get a ladder.

Sitting on Soraya's little stool behind the counter, I pulled on the six-hundred-reduced-to-three-hundred-dollar boots. I didn't hate for a second that they had at least five-inch heels. "Fierce!" I gasped. I stood and headed
5 for the mirror.

As I turned back and forth in the mirror, getting the front and the back view, it hit me. I took a moment. I wanted to be sure it came out exactly right.

"Soraya, honey," I started.

10 "You don't even have half the money, so don't even think about it. And besides, I told you, they're girls'!"

"How could you work in this place and be so backward, Soraya? I mean, really! I'm embarrassed for you! Who is separating men's from women's clothes anymore? It's not
15 like I tried on a bra! They're boots! Black, fabulous boots that fit me and make my legs look incredible and make me look like a star, and that's all that matters. That's what all clothes are supposed to do. They don't define whether you can give birth or not! Now, if you are really my friend and
20 have any fashion sense at all, you will admit how *beyond excellent* these look on me, and you will do me a huge, huge favor!"

"No!" Soraya said as soon as I'd gotten the r in "favor" out of my mouth.

25 "But you don't even know what I'm asking."

"If it has anything to do with those boots leaving the store without you giving me three hundred dollars, the answer is no. No!"

I didn't once take my eyes off myself in the boots. I
30 stood firmly in them as though they'd been designed for me and I was reunited with them at last.

"Soraya, what I want you to do is to be calm and listen to me. This is me, Carlos. Your friend. I am dependable. Trustworthy. Smart. And I'm going to be rich enough one day to buy four pairs of these in one shopping trip without
5 even thinking twice about it. So I want you to really pay attention to who is asking you what I'm about to ask you."

"Darling, I know who is about to ask me something. You are Carlos Duarte, and you're a crazy person. And I don't even want to hear it."

10 I had no choice but to get it out fast. "Soraya, I want you to let me wear these just for the interview, which means a couple of hours. Not a day, not a half day. A couple of *hours*. I will wear some other shoes to the store, change into the Stellas in the men's room, and only wear
15 them for my interview. When the interview is over, I will go back to the men's room—"

"In my store's ladies' boots!"

"And change into my own shoes. I may be crazy, but I'm honest, and you know it. Please. I would *so* do it for
20 you. I promise on my life—no, on my *career*—that I won't let anything happen to them. Please. I will never ask you for anything ever again. Please." I stopped and posed in the boots.

"I caaaannnn't, Carlos. I caaaannn't."

25 I sat down again and took the boots off as quickly as I could. Standing in my socks, holding them against my chest, I pleaded in almost a whisper. "I swear I'll come in the same day, just before I have to go for my interview, and come back right afterward." I took a step closer and
30 leaned toward her. "I know these will help me get the job, Soraya. I know it. I knew it as soon as I saw them. Of course, if I had the money like some of the rich kids who

26

come in here and just throw down their credit cards, I would do it. But I can't." Then I had an idea. "Do you want me to give you money? I could!" Soraya looked horrified. "I could give you maybe a hundred dollars if I save it from
5 my pay, and then when I bring them back and they're exactly the same as when I left, you could give me my hundred dollars back!"

"Carlos! I can't believe you thought of that!" Soraya scrunched up her face and looked pretty unattractive
10 doing it. "No, I wouldn't take your money. I wouldn't. I'm just so afraid…"

But I knew she was closer than she had been at the beginning.

"I know you're afraid. Because you're a responsible
15 person. And that's why you're a good manager. And I respect that. That's why I wouldn't do anything to screw that up. I swear." I made my voice even lower and more vulnerable-sounding. "Soraya, if I let anything happen to these boots, you have every right to never speak to me
20 again. Plus, you'll have my hundred dollars."

"I told you already, Carlos, I wouldn't take your money. No offense. I just mean, how could I? We're supposed to be friends." She sighed this incredibly deep sigh. "I have to think about it. I have to."

25 I knew to keep my mouth shut. I quietly put my sneakers back on and wiped the toes of the boots with my hands, gently, signaling to Soraya how valuable I knew the Stella McCartneys were. "I guess I'll go. You let me know… what you decide." I turned and started slowly toward the
30 door.

Before I could open it, she said, "Oh, you're such a little actor, Carlos! How am I supposed to say no to you!"

27

I swung around not quite believing it was happening.

"But you know you could get me fired, don't you? And I need this job!"

"I won't do one single thing to jeopardize your job,
Soraya, not one single thing!"

"And you have to keep your word. You pick them up the day of, and you don't put them on until before the interview, and you take them off immediately after, and you bring them the bloody hell here as soon as you can!"

I loved her when she tried to use her fake British accent. It was so fake and so awful, but I'd seen her use it on customers, and they fell for it.

"I bloody will!" I said, sounding like Queen Elizabeth herself. I hugged the boots, and she grabbed them from me. "Don't touch these until you come back for your appointment!"

"I adore you, Soraya. I truly do adore you and your fake British ass!"

I left Tokyo Jo's thinking it almost didn't matter what else I walked up to the FeatureFace counter wearing. I'd have on thigh-high Stella McCartney boots, looking like I'd designed the makeup for anybody I said I had. FeatureFace better be ready. Carrlos Duarte was coming. They just better be ready. That was if, of course, they ever called me.

CHAPTER 5

Friday morning it happened. I was in history class when my thigh vibrated.

I got up and ran out, even though it's totally against the rules. "Hello, hello!" I shouted in the hallway.

5 "This is Valentino, the manager of FeatureFace Cosmetics at Macy's." He said it like he was saying, *This is Meryl Streep, and I've been nominated for a zillion Oscars.* "Is Carlos Duarte there?"

"This is Carlos," I said, trying to sound like Meryl too, 10 except in *The Devil Wears Prada.*

"We want to see you tomorrow for an interview. We have two slots available. An eleven and a one thirty."

As soon as he got out "One thirty," I said, "Eleven."

"Fine. Bring your résumé and a model for your makeup 15 demonstration."

"Of course," I said, like it was old, old information for a pro like me.

"Don't be late. We have a very full schedule on Saturday and we don't tolerate lateness." Now *he* was definitely 20 Meryl in *Prada.*

"I won't. I'm never late," I babbled. "Thank you." But he didn't hear any of it, because he'd already hung up.

I started the conversation with myself right then and there. Everyone has these conversations, I know, and 25 usually people say conversations with yourself are in people's minds, but that's not true with me. Because it always feels like the conversation is traveling through my whole body. If it's going one way, it stays in my head for a while before it moves on. Sometimes it goes to my throat really quickly and my throat gets tight, or into my heart, or my heart and my throat at the same time, but all the parts answer one way or another. And this conversation about the model for my test, who it should be and what I should do with her, filled my head and my stomach and my heart, hands, legs, ankles, and feet.

As soon as I got out of school, I started toward Burrito Take-Out Village. I wasn't sure all the time what Rosalia's schedule was, but I knew if she wasn't there, she'd be there soon. I'd wait outside. But, as it turned out, I didn't have to. God knew I had important business to take care of.

My sister was there. She looked at me standing inside the door. Then, she came over and asked me, "What's up?"

Of course, when she spoke to me, Danny looked up from the grill. He turned his head away from both of us to the kitchen and said something in a squeaky voice. Rosalia was trying to pretend she wasn't hearing it.

I said, "I wanted to tell you something, but I think maybe it's not a good time."

There were more voices coming out of the kitchen and then these squeals.

She looked at me, and I could see she was frustrated. "I'm sorry, Carlos. They're idiots. What can I say?"

I made a face in their direction even though I couldn't see any of them.

"I'll see you at home, Rosalia."

Immediately I heard from the kitchen, "See-you-at-home-Rosalia!"

Rosalia turned and yelled back, "Yoouu guuuys!" But I was on my way out of there.

CHAPTER 6

Okay, historic day requires historic look, yes? It only makes sense. So, black almost-skinny jeans, which Angie says make me look like I have mosquito legs, only from the knees down. Like she knows what mosquito legs look like.
5 Black pin-striped men's suit jacket cut like it's from the thirties. It lost the pinstripes because I dyed it, but I still love the way it fits.

I also had on my red sneakers, which would come off as soon as I got to Macy's, just like I'd promised Soraya-Anna-
10 Wintour. Under my arm, a red vinyl combination book bag and binder. I used it to carry my fake résumé and the pictures Gleason had taken of my own version of *America's Next Top Model*—from the neck up anyway. The vinyl bag was actually for a kid, but I swear I could have passed it off
15 as a Gucci original.

Three fingertips full of gel in my hair so it looked shower fresh. My eyes were clear. I had just the slightest touch of color in my cheeks. I'd given myself a manicure. I looked *beyond excellent*!
20 I was arriving at Macy's without my model. When I finally got to tell Rosalia I'd picked her to come with me and be my model, she acted as though I'd asked her to loan me money. "All right," she sighed, "but Saturday is our busiest day at my job. I really shouldn't, but I'll go
25 there on Saturday morning and tell them I have an emergency and I'll be back in the afternoon."

I hated that she was making it very clear it was this big sacrifice, so I said, "I'll pay you for the hour I need you,

Rosalia, I swear." And with Rosalia, money changes everything, so she said yes.

Our agreement was that she would meet me at the Thirty-fourth Street entrance to Macy's, but when I started
5 walking toward the store, I could see she wasn't there.

"Please, please, Rosalia, don't mess this up for me," I was praying, waiting outside the store.

But I had to go inside and change into my boots and at least check out where the counter was so I wouldn't be
10 late for my interview. "Rosalia," I said under my breath, "I will never forgive you for this!"

As soon as I got into the store, there was a guard, and I asked where the nearest men's room was. He mumbled something about the second floor or the basement, giving
15 me this once-over that I didn't appreciate. *I mean, it's New York. Haven't you seen every kind of person there is in this city?* But I just followed his mumble and got on the escalator to the second floor. I don't do basements. Besides, I figured from the second floor I could get a helicopter view of the
20 first floor and see where FeatureFace was.

The first floor was actually like Cosmetics Counters City. The whole area looked like there was an army of men and women in black guarding Cosmetics Counters City. They walked slowly through the aisles, staring out at the
25 customers, or they stood behind the counters, glancing at themselves in the mirrors. Some of them were armed with perfumes or creams. Once I saw the FeatureFace counter, I couldn't take my eyes off it. It had this big sign that spelled out "FeatureFace" in makeup mirror bulbs.

30 I found the men's room and took off my red sneakers. Pulled the Stellas out and pulled them up my thighs. I was *superb-ia* and I knew it. Just the five-inch heels alone were

32

enough to make me feel like FeatureFace should be happy I was applying for the job.

When I came out, I checked my cell. Four minutes to eleven and no message from Rosalia. *If she's not here, I may as well take these boots off and get right back on the train.* I was sweating. It was probably my imagination, but it felt like the Stella McCartneys were sweating too.

I went toward the escalator. I looked down at the first floor, toward the Cosmetics Counters City. I looked at the FeatureFace counter. Ohmygod! There was Rosalia, standing there with her coat over her arm in some very tight pants and a horrible orange and white fuzzy sweater that made her look like a big calico cat. And her hair was so humungous, it looked like she'd just escaped from a shock therapy session. But she was there!

I raced down the escalator trying to look like I was floating—but floating fast! I got to the FeatureFace counter without knowing how I got through the army of black uniforms and the thick screen of perfume and makeup.

"Hi," I said into Rosalia's neck, hugging her.

"Scared ya, didn't I? But I told ya I was coming!"

I pulled myself together and looked at her. "I thought I told you to come without any makeup on!"

Rosalia frowned at me like I'd said, "I thought I told you to come without any clothes on!"

"Well, that wasn't going to happen," she snipped.

"May I help you with something today?" a voice chirped behind us.

I whirled around, and there was a girl with enough hair weave to compete in the Miss Black Rapunzel Contest. She was gorgeous, except for the green contacts, and I wanted to tell her she could do without about four feet of the weave, but instead I told her, "I have an interview with Valentino at eleven."

"Okay, hon," Miss Rapunzel chirped. She couldn't fling her hair because there was too much of it, hanging down the front and back of her black blouse. Off she went around the corner of the counter, and I took the time to take deep breaths and compose myself.

I could hear voices behind the counter, but I couldn't see who they belonged to. Just mumbling. More mumbling. Then Miss Rapunzel came back into view. "Valentino will be right out," she said cheerily.

"No, Valentino said he was busy and would come out as soon as he could," came this voice like the Wizard of Oz from behind the curtain. I was pretty sure from the sound of it that I'd better take a few more deep breaths.

Miss Rapunzel shrugged and laughed. She whispered, "Well, you heard him."

I smiled big because I wanted her to know I'd be fun to work with. "I'm Carlos, and this is my sis—this is Rosalia." I'd decided not to say that Rosalia was related to me, especially now with her in the stretch pants and the calico cat sweater. I wasn't ashamed of my sister. I was embarrassed that I didn't have a professional model and that the one I had looked like she was posing for a "Fashion Don't" column. Any other day but this one.

I saw his head first, then the top part of his body, then the bottom. In sections. He was a giraffe in a black V-neck sweater, black pants, and about thirty silver bracelets, fifteen on each arm.

He moved toward me in slow—very slow—motion. Can people be seven feet tall, with no fat on any part of their bodies? Pale, pale skin with two spots of pink on his

cheeks that couldn't be real. His eyes were big black marbles with long black fringe framing them. His cinnamon hair stood out in every direction and still curled at the ends, so it was like a halo that shined under the fluorescent
5 lights.

He was looking in our direction, but he didn't seem to be looking at us. He was looking over our heads, so when he stopped in front of us, I almost turned around to see what it was he was staring at.

10 "I'm Valentino," he announced. And he still wasn't looking at me or my sister.

"I'm Carrlos Duarte," I said as though I'd said it hundreds of times in professional situations, "and this is my model, Rosalia."

15 He looked down somewhat, but he still never focused on me. "Where have you worked before?"

I put my red book bag on the counter and quickly unzipped it. "I have my résumé here," I said, suddenly out of breath as though I'd run ten miles to get there.

20 "Just tell me where the last place you worked was. As a makeup artist." His voice sounded like a stapler.

"Well, I go to school, so I haven't done it full-time. But I…" I was stalling, trying to think of a name to give him. Of course I'd practiced it, but I hadn't ever imagined the
25 creature in front of me asking the question. "I worked on Saturdays and holidays at Bobby's, downtown."

"Bobby'sdowntown?" Still looking over the top of my head, he said it like it was one clearly made-up word. "And you say you're in school?"

30 "Yes, but I'm only applying for part-time right now. And Christmas."

"And other than this… Bobby's…" Valentino stared at my fake résumé like a bird had crapped on it. "I don't recognize any of these… places."

Just then Miss Rapunzel rushed up to Valentino. "Craig Denton is here, Val. He came in the other side. He asked where you were."

I immediately saw a change in Valentino, and I was thrilled to hear that Miss Rapunzel had cut his name to "Val," which I was sure I would someday. But who was Craig Denton?

"Our account executive is here today visiting. Couldn't have happened at a busier time," Valentino said, and sniffed. He put my résumé on the counter. "Why don't you get ready to work with your model, so I can see what you did at… Bobby's. I'll be back. Lissette will get you whatever you tell her you need."

As he turned to go, I saw the top of what must have been Craig Denton's shaved head somewhere behind the counter. And Valentino went to the person I guessed must have been his boss. "Oh," he said over his shoulder, "I want a Sunday brunch look. Then you will take it to a nighttime club look. I hope you learned how to do that at… Bobby's. And I'm hoping you weren't responsible for the makeup she's already wearing, because it's definitely *not* what we do at FeatureFace." I glared at my sister, who was busy rolling her horrifically made-up eyes at the man I hoped was going to be my future boss.

As soon as he was gone, Lissette Rapunzel asked softly, as though I was trying to light a brand-new gas oven with a book of matches, "Have you ever done this before?"

"Yes," I lied breezily. "Of course."

"You should just keep talking to me, telling me every-thing you're doing," she whispered. "When Valentino comes back, just keep talking. And don't forget to sell the product, baby!"

5   I turned Rosalia toward me like she was a life-size doll. "The first thing I'd like to do is give your face a good cleansing." I felt like I was doing an infomercial, which I guess I was. "We'll get rid of all this makeup, which I *didn't* put on"—I said loudly—"and we can start fresh! Lissette,
10 do we have any of FeatureFace's Softwipes and their special Earth-friendly Gel Cleanser?" *Thank God for the Internet.* I'd done my homework, and I'd talk just loud enough to impress Lissette and so that Valentino could hear me a few feet away.

15   Lissette was giggling. She went to get the cleanser and the Softwipes.

"Why are you talking so loud?" Rosalia snapped. "You're embarrassing me!"

"It's not *for* you," I snapped back. "I know what I'm
20 doing, so just please this once keep quiet!"

Lissette came back and put the cleanser and Softwipes on the counter next to me. "Thank you, Lissette. By the way, I love your hair."

I was used to using my fingers for everything. But when
25 I started to rub the concealer under Rosalia's eye, Lissette made a sound like she was choking, so I got the hint. "FeatureFace also has these wonderful brushes you can use. No one uses their fingers anymore," I said, and Lissette couldn't stop herself from laughing.

30   A few minutes later I could hear Valentino talking to Craig Denton as I got to Rosalia's eye shadow. They were coming toward us. I was feeling so good, I got even louder.

"Now I'm going to use FeatureFace's incredible Perfect Pink as the base. You can see it's a subtle, more neutral pink—which my customers love—and we're using it to hold our color down. And we'll put a deeper, richer pink on top. I'm going to put a nice medium brown in the crease, keeping it subtle. Remember, it's your daytime look, so subtlety is the key." I stole that last bit directly from a *Vogue* article I'd read last fall about daytime makeup.

Valentino and Craig Denton were now right behind Lissette! They'd stopped talking, and both of them were watching me.

"The thing that's so great about FeatureFace's shadows is how they create so much dimension with such little effort!" I had no idea what I was saying, really. It was everything I'd ever studied mixed with every ad and commercial for makeup I'd ever seen.

"You're very good for someone so young. How long have you been working for us?" I kept brushing Rosalia's eyelids, not able to speak. Was this guy really speaking to me? *How long have you been working for us?*

"He doesn't." Valentino sounded dry, but not as dry as he had when he'd been talking to me. Not at all. "This is an interview. I'm not sure he has as much experience as we'd like."

"Oh, come on," Craig Denton said, and I could tell he was smiling even though I was too nervous to look at him. "He obviously knows what he's doing. And he's definitely a good salesman."

"Yes," Valentino said in this tone that could have been agreeing to having his cavities drilled.

"I'll be curious to see what this looks like when you're finished—what is your name?"

"Carrlos Duarte," I said, wishing I could have announced it in the voice I used when I was daydreaming something like this was happening.

"Well, if I'm still here, Lissette, you come get me."

5   "Absolutely, Craig," Lissette bubbled.

"I'm not sure you *will* still be here, Craig." Valentino sighed. "He's going *very* slowly. As far as I'm concerned, he should have finished the first look already—"

"You know, Val, speed is something that comes with
10 time. When he's been doing it for as long as you have"— Craig Denton chuckled—"I'm sure he'll be as fast as you are." Valentino's mouth did this puckering thing that looked like he was tasting the words "for as long as you have," and they didn't taste good at all.

15   "Fine," Valentino snapped. "When he's finally finished the first look, Lissette, let us know." And they went around the corner to another part of the FeatureFace counter.

As soon as they'd gone, Rosalia squealed, "Ooo, Carlos!"

"Do you know how fabulous that is?" Lissette said.

20   "Who is he?" I asked.

"Craig Denton, the Manager of Retail Operations. And he oversees all the FeatureFace retail outlets in the city. He started on the floor, then was a counter manager like Valentino, then got promoted to MRO."

25   "And does it matter if he likes what I'm doing?"

"Let's put it this way: If he likes what he sees, Valentino would have to explain why he *didn't* hire you."

"Then why is Valentino being soooo…" I wasn't sure I should say exactly what I was thinking. But I really didn't
30 understand why he wasn't being any friendlier.

"If you get the job, honey, we can go have tea and I'll give you all the dirt. But for now just work fast so you can get employed!"

I started to paint Rosalia's face like we were on the subway tracks, a train was coming, and neither one of us could escape till her makeup was done. From eyeliner I went to mascara, and from mascara I went to lipstick moisturizer, and as I finished her lip gloss, I told Lissette, "All right, go tell 'em they can come take a look!"

In the few minutes Lissette was gone, I checked and rechecked Rosalia's face. Valentino would have to admit it wasn't at all the girl he'd seen when I started.

When Lissette led Val and his boss back, I pretended I was just putting on some finishing touches.

"See, I was right. The kid has some talent!" Craig Denton stood there in front of Rosalia.

"You know, Craig," Valentino drawled, "this is still only half of what is required. Usually, as you know, there are *two* looks—"

"Yes, I do. And since it seems to be taking us a considerable amount of time to look at your totals, I'll no doubt be here when his second look is done." He turned to Lissette. "Come get us, would you?"

Valentino was boiling. "It will take us no time at all, I'm sure. Juan—"

"Carlos!" I shot my correction back at him. *Don't even try that with me.*

Valentino looked shocked at my tone. "Carlos. You have twenty minutes to complete the nighttime look. Thank you."

It was exactly eighteen minutes later when Valentino and Mr. Denton came back. I remember because Lissette announced when it was seventeen minutes, and I still hadn't put any lip gloss on Rosalia. When I heard the two of them coming, I decided to leave it rather than look like I hadn't finished on time.

5 "I see you managed," Mr. Denton said, "and from what I can see, I'm pretty impressed."

I was just about to thank him when Valentino said, "Well, I'm *still* concerned about how slow he is. If there was a line here on a Saturday, we'd be in big trouble."

10 Mr. Denton said calmly, "I understand your concern, Valentino."

"And, frankly, I don't think the references are quite up to our standards."

Mr. Denton looked at me from head to toe. I couldn't 15 have been more grateful at that moment for my Stella McCartneys. I was tempted to ease casually into a ballet position that showed them off more, but I thought it might be too much.

"Do you have a portfolio, Carlos?"

20 "Of course, Mr. Denton," I said, reaching over to the counter to get my bag. I heard Mr. Denton chuckle, and I knew both my Stellas and my red vinyl had scored.

Opening to my pictures, I said, "Obviously, this is just a sample of my work." I suddenly wished I had thirty more 25 photos, with layouts from *Bazaar* or *Teen Vogue* or at least a Kmart catalogue!

Valentino sniped, "There's not a lot of variety. Looks like they were all done by the same photographer. Probably at the same shoot." I thought about a TV commercial 30 where a little boy eats glue and can't open his mouth to speak. That's what I fantasized about the mean giraffe in the V-neck sweater and the thirty bracelets.

41

"Still, it's good work," Mr. Denton said. He looked from Rosalia's picture to her. "Is this the same model?"

"Yes," we both said. Actually, Rosalia kind of shouted "Yeah!" and grinned. I flashed her a look that said, *Don't say. One. Single. Word.*

Mr. Denton stepped back and stared at me. I stared right back. *Go on. Do it. Hire me. It's the best decision you'll ever make!*

He said, "I think this is someone we want to give a chance, Val. Just as you were given a chance… and I was given a chance before you."

With the five of us in the same small area, it seemed like there wasn't a sound.

Finally Mr. Denton broke the silence. "What's the worst that could happen? I'm sure our young friend here knows that if he can't keep up, we can't afford to keep him on salary. Don't you, Carlos?"

I turned to both of them. "I know I can keep up."

There was another big, long silence. I knew I'd said all I could say, and I was hoping Rosalia had sense enough to keep her mouth shut. Lissette had made herself practically invisible, and all I could concentrate on were Valentino and Craig Denton. *Please, God. Please.*

"Well, if you're that impressed, Craig," Valentino drawled.

"I am," Mr. Denton said, and I put my hand on Rosalia's knee and squeezed it hard. Rosalia put hers over mine and clamped it like she was Mickey Rourke in *The Wrestler*.

"Then, I guess it's settled." Valentino looked like he was at a dinner party and hated everything on his plate, but all he could do was smile and try to get some of it down.

"Welcome," Craig Denton said to me, and put out his hand. I wanted to hug him, but I wasn't *that* crazy.

"Thank you very much, Mr. Denton."

"Please don't call me Mr. Denton. It makes me feel about seventy-five years old. And, just so you know, you are now working for the most dynamic cosmetics firm in the industry," he told me in this honey-dripping baritone. "Not only do we have one of the strongest retail lines in the world, but we also have a huge celebrity client base. Once you get some real education on the line, I'm sure you'll be very impressed."

"I'm impressed already," I told him. I was trying to imitate his baritone honey drip. I gave him my biggest Carrlos Duarte, celebrity-in-training smile. And I could see Valentino, the giraffe in the V-neck sweater, rolling his big black marble eyes up toward the Macy's chandeliers.

CHAPTER 7

I was in shock. I could hardly think. And Rosalia kept shrieking, "Man, Carlos, I can't believe it!"

Valentino told me, "I'll call you with the date you're going to start working." He said it like it hurt. I thanked him so much for giving me the opportunity—yeah, right. Craig Denton had already disappeared.

When me and Rosalia were going through the revolving doors on the way out—I'm not gonna lie—I remember realizing that I still had on the Stella McCartneys. It was just for a second, but I did think of it. But I couldn't go back into the store to take them off. Not then. Not when all the cameras in my head were watching *Carlos Duarte, Newly Hired Macy's Makeup Artist, and His Model-Sister, Rosalia, Leaving the World Famous Department Store.* How could I stop, go back into the men's room, and change into a pair of dirty sneakers at a moment like that?

I went with Rosalia from the store to the subway practically without realizing how I got there. We kept going over all the details, and I was really glad that she was the one who'd been there. She was family, and it meant a lot to me that she was my sister.

"I have to go right to work and hope I'm not fired," she said. That's what brought me back to reality.

"You won't be, hon," I told her. "Today is too special. Nothing can go wrong, I swear."

At Fourteenth Street, when Rosalia got off the train, I gave her a kiss on the cheek. "You're right," I told her. "If I hadn't had you there, it would never have gone the way it did."

At Eighth Street, when I got off the train, I started daydreaming again about every detail of what happened at the store. I walked all the way to the end of the platform, talking to myself, repeating everything that Craig Denton had said about me to Valentino.

When I got to the bottom of the stairs, I looked up and saw Danny. Behind him were his two friends from Burrito Take-Out Village coming down toward me.

"Hi," I said softly to Danny. He didn't say anything. I started up the stairs. I tripped on something and glanced down to see what it was. It looked like a rusty curtain rod. I moved aside so that the guys could pass. I looked up again at Danny. So he was going to ignore me. He was my

44

sister's boyfriend, but he wasn't even going to try to force a fake "hi" just for her sake.

As they got closer, I could smell liquor on them. One of them said, "Oooooh, Carrrloooss!" in this really girly voice. Danny was already next to me. One of the others was standing above me on the stairs. He spit down at me. I backed up, trying to get away. I fell, and the spit hit the front of my jacket anyway. Danny and the other kid started laughing.

I was half lying, half sitting on the subway stairs glaring up at my sister's boyfriend. I wasn't scared. I was mad.

It wasn't as though I didn't know them. I knew where they worked, and I could bring a cop there in a second. Was he crazy? Were they all crazy? Danny reached down. I froze. Danny grabbed the curtain rod and handed it to his friend. It was like he was giving him instructions that didn't need to be said out loud. The guy took the rod and pulled it up one of my boots, scratching the smooth black leather from the toe all the way up the thigh. I grabbed the end of it and tried to jump up and get out of his way, but I wasn't fast enough. "You stupid piece of garbage!" I screamed. "You piece of crap!"

Someone was on their way up the stairs. The guys all ran past me, laughing and calling my name. "Carrrloooss! Carrrloooss!" I only knew one of their names—Danny's— but it didn't matter. I could see all of their faces, and I knew where to find them. And I wasn't sure exactly what I'd do. But I had to do something. I looked down at the ruined boots I should have taken off like I'd sworn I would. I wiped the spit off the front of my jacket with my sleeve.

At home I tried to think of how I could fix the scratch before I took the boots back to Soraya. But when I saw how deep and long it was, I realized there was no way anybody was gonna pay three hundred dollars for those boots anymore, Stella McCartneys or not. And besides that, I would have done anything not to face Soraya. What could I say? I wore them out of the store like I'd promised I wouldn't, and then I got them destroyed by a friend of my sister's boyfriend?

And that's exactly what I *did* say to Soraya. No matter how it happened, the boots were ruined. So I just told Soraya the truth. I finished by saying, "All I can do is say if you give me enough time, I can pay for them. But it will be a while, even with my new job."

Soraya couldn't have cared less about my new job, which was understandable, since now she was worried about losing hers.

"What do you think this is, Carlos? We don't do layaway! It's not that kind of store. You come back here with ruined boots that I let you take out of here, and you expect me to put you on a payment plan? You're living in a bigger fantasy world than I thought! I trusted you!"

"I'm really sorry, Soraya. I know I let you down, and I know you probably hate me. But all I can do is offer to pay for the boots. And if I had three hundred dollars right now, I'd give it to you. But I don't."

"So all you can do is apologize—I got it. Now, could you please leave the store, Carlos? I have customers."

She said it like she didn't know me. And I just hoped she wouldn't be fired because of me.

I walked out of Tokyo Jo's and glanced down at my jacket and remembered how excited Soraya had been when she'd told me she could sell it to me for so much less because it was a little faded. Today some guy had spit on it.

And in a way I felt like I'd done the same to my friendship with Soraya.

CHAPTER 8

Before I could say anything, Rosalia came home from work and started. "I just had the worst afternoon of my life, the worst! It started off just fine with you, Carlos, and then I get to work and I'm in a perfectly good mood. And then they tell me Danny, Juan, and Oscar are all fired."

She didn't wait for me to say anything. "There was money missing from the cash register, and Tina, the girl who was working for me, said she had just counted an hour before that and she wasn't short, so Miguel goes off and fires Danny, Juan, and Oscar on the spot. I call Danny every chance I get and he's not answering his phone." She plopped down onto the couch with her face to the ceiling and her hands over her face.

Ma said, "Well, maybe he's not answering because he feels guilty," and Rosalia went nuts. "Thanks, Ma. Thank you very much. I know you don't like him and you don't even know him. So now he's a thief?"

"I'm just saying, why won't he answer his phone and talk to you if he's so innocent?"

And that's when I knew I wasn't going to tell what happened with Danny and these other two guys. But I did ask Rosalia to repeat their names, because when I did decide to do whatever I was going to do about them, I'd at least have all of their freaking names.

47

"I'm not saying they're thieves, Rosalia, but I do agree with Ma that it's weird the guy won't return your phone calls if he doesn't have anything to hide."

And when Rosalia gave me a dirty look and said, "How can you be so unsympathetic? You got everything you wanted today, didn't you?" I thought *I really should just tell her right now.* But then she started crying and said, "It's like you always say, Carlos. You're gonna be famous and have money and a good life. And I'm always gonna be stuck with some guy that people think is a thief or a drug addict or some other dirtbag."

And, yes, I did think he was trash. And that's exactly what I wanted to tell my sister. But I didn't. Because, yeah, the day started out great and I couldn't be happier about getting hired by FeatureFace. But I also probably lost a friend because I was a big liar and I didn't keep my word. So I couldn't make myself tell my sister that her boyfriend and his friends attacked me and they probably did steal the money at her job. I just couldn't.

But I *did* tell Angie. She said I should go to the police and report what she kept calling "an assault." When she started calling the curtain rod a deadly weapon, I told her she should get a job writing for *Law and Order.*

I'm not going to report it," I told her. "If those pigs are arrested for stealing from that stupid burrito stand, it will be justice enough. I hope the cops put them in the Tombs for seventy-five years."

"Yeah," Angie said. "That's if the owner even presses charges."

"How could he not press charges?"

"People get fired for stealing all the time," Angie said like she was the theft authority, "and people don't press

charges. How much could they have stolen from a burrito take-out register? A hundred dollars? I betcha nothing happens, Carlos. And didn't you say Danny was one of the cooks and the others were just kitchen helpers? Then he
5 could say it was them and keep his job. You watch."

For the next few days I waited for Rosalia to come home from work and say her boss was pressing charges against Danny. Instead she texted me one day and told me exactly what Angie had predicted. Her text said, "thank
10 Gd. D tld Miguel he dint steal the mny. he sys one of the otr giys did it. Mig sd d cld cme bac!!! im sooo hppy."

I guess that day there was good news for both of us. Lissette called from Macy's and told me Valentino wanted me to come to work the next Saturday. I called Angie and
15 told her.

We went to the Thai Palace on Fourteenth Street to celebrate. She almost ruined the night by bugging me to tell Rosalia what happened in the subway station. "I always thought you had more guts than to let something like this
20 happen to you and not do anything!"

I tried to bring the focus of the night back to where it should be—on me and my future as a makeup star.

"Angie," I said, "do you remember the first time you dared me to put on a full face of makeup to go to the
25 movies, and I did?"

"Of course." She laughed. "We got into a fight because people kept staring, and you said, 'What did you expect? I'm beautiful.' And I said you overdid it because you knew people would stare."

30 "Then you said," I reminded Angie, "'Well, you must have been putting on makeup since you were born.' And I

said, 'Angie girl, I've been putting makeup on the fat boy for a very long time.'"

Angie was laughing at the memory. And I told her, "Well, now someone is paying the fat boy to put makeup on *other* people. And it's only the beginning!"

But she still couldn't get over the story about Danny and the run-in on the subway stairs. "You're gonna be sorry if you don't do something about it, Carlos. Just trust me. I can feel it."

And I told my friend, "Angie, please just eat your fried rice and think only good thoughts!"

But the whole time we sat there, it was true I never stopped picturing the guy standing over me, dragging that curtain rod up my boot and spitting on me.

CHAPTER 9

Walking into school, I heard this voice I didn't recognize at first. "Carlos?"

When I turned, I still didn't see where the voice was coming from. I lowered my sunglasses a bit, to get a better look, but there were about four kids I talked to in the whole school, including Angie, and I swear I didn't see any of them.

"Carlos."

I actually jumped and made this little shriek.

"Sorry I scared you. I was calling you, and you turned around and looked right at me."

"I did? I'm sorry, Gleason. I did hear somebody calling me. I just wasn't sure where it was coming from." He had on the tightest red T-shirt with a faded black-and-white photo of Jimi Hendrix on it. Black skinny jeans and black work boots open, with the laces hanging like he'd just gotten out of bed and slipped them on at the last minute. It was the gray eyes, though, that got me every time.

"I wanted to ask you something," he said.

"Anything." I smiled, and stared at him from behind my dark glasses.

"I'm thinking about putting some of the photographs I took for you in a show I got in, and I wanted to get your okay."

"A show? You're gonna put them in a photography show? When is it? Of course it's okay! What are you, crazy? *You* took them—they're as much yours as they are mine! You certainly don't have to ask me!"

I was completely stunned. I knew he was in the photography club, and I also knew he took great photographs, but I didn't think he was that serious or that ambitious. But then, I also didn't know him half as well as I wanted to.

He pulled his hand slowly through his curls, kind of tugging at them. It was *beyond sexy*—the boy was truly dangerous. "I only got a chance to take the model shots because you asked me to," he said. "But when the guy who put me in the show saw all my pictures, he said I should definitely include them. He said it showed that I had a good eye for more than rock concerts and bands."

"And is this your first show?"

"Yeah. This... uh... friend of mine, Gabrielle, knows somebody who works in this gallery, and they were doing this show that's supposedly new talent that they think is gonna be big someday. Gabs got her friend to show her boss, the guy who runs the gallery, my stuff…" Gleason shrugged shyly. "I guess he thought I fit that description."

I wanted to tell Gleason Kraft just how many descriptions I thought he fit, but I didn't.

5 "So am I invited to the opening?" I asked him. "Or is it only for celebrities and the press?" Of course, in my mind, I was definitely a celebrity even if only Angie and me knew it.

"Yeah, sure you are, if you want to. I don't really know 10 anything about the opening yet. But if I can invite people, then, sure."

"What do you mean *if* you can invite people? It's your show, isn't it?"

"Naw," he said, laughing. "I just told you, it's a *group* 15 show. There are about seven other people, I think."

"I'm really happy for you, Gleason. And I'm glad I asked you to do my pictures."

It was then that two of his rocker buddies called him, and everything about him was different. He sounded 20 different, his face wasn't as alive and warm as before, the way he was standing changed. It was odd, and it was a little sad, I thought. Because I'd never seen the Gleason I was talking to before, really. I'd seen glimpses of him when we were doing the shoots, but today talking about his 25 show, he was all there. And then suddenly he was gone.

But don't think for a minute that I didn't start to daydream about it right then in the hall. I didn't have all the details, but I definitely could see me entering the gallery. Gleason came right over and grabbed a glass of 30 champagne from the nearest waiter and said, "I didn't think you were coming," in this voice that sounded like Jeremy Irons. And I smiled and looked at the photographs.

They were billboard-size and underneath were these signs that said, THESE PHOTOS ARE DEDICATED TO CARRLOS DUARTE, BECAUSE WITHOUT HIM THEY WOULDN'T EXIST.

"Carlos?"

5   I heard Angie, and I really didn't want to come out of the daydream. Especially to be in the reality of Sojourner Truth/John F. Kennedy Freedom High School at eight thirty on a Tuesday morning.

"Hi, hon."

10   "What was Gleason talking about?"

"Oh, that." I pulled my glasses down onto my nose to look at her with raised eyebrows, and I said, "Angie, I don't think I realized it before, but I think I have a... a thing for Gleason Kraft."

15   At this point Angie got very, very loud. She screamed with laughter.

"What is so funny, Angie? You're embarrassing me!"

"I can't believe you're trying to tell me you didn't realize you had a thing for Gleason Kraft!"

20   Now I'm paranoid that she made an announcement to the entire student body. She may as well have been handing out leaflets.

"Would you keep your voice down, pleeeez! I really don't get what the big joke is!"

25   "There is no joke. I just can't believe that as smart as you're supposed to be, how come you're the last to get that you have a thing for Gleason Kraft!"

And I couldn't answer her. Because what she didn't know was that what I was really saying was I never *admit-*
30 *ted* to myself that I was infatuated with Gleason Kraft before. But the fact was, the Gleason I saw *before* he disappeared, the Gleason who called to me and told me about

his show, made me think that maybe I might get a chance to... to what? I didn't know. But the *chance* part. That's what was important.

CHAPTER 10

When I left the human resources office of Macy's and went
5 down to the first floor as an official FeatureFace employee, Lissette announced to me, "Val's gonna be late as usual. Only I'm not supposed to tell you he's late, of course. But I am supposed to show you where everything is and in between you should jump right in and see if you can make
10 any sales."

And that was the name of the game—SALES.

Lissette explained, "I don't know where else you've worked doing this, but for this company it's about customer satisfaction and sales."

15 I was nodding.

"We've had so-called makeup artists come in here, and they think it's all about putting on the makeup. So they spend hours and hours putting on the makeup and chatting and at the end the customer gets up, looks in the mirror,
20 sometimes says 'Thank you' and then, gone! And what have we sold? Nothing! And do you think Valentino is happy about that? No! Because at the end of the day, Craig Denton, the manager of retail operations, wants those numbers, and Valentino has to give 'em up. We are all
25 responsible, but Valentino's butt is on the line!"

"I understand," I told her. I was glad she was telling me this and not Valentino, because it made me understand what I didn't know about the business and, more important, what Val wanted from me.

"Now, the thing about Valentino is, he may come in late, leave early, take a long lunch. But when he needs to make the numbers, nobody can sell like he can. And because he's a makeup artist, he can demonstrate, too." She said, lowering her voice a little, "Me, I got plenty of mouth and charm and sex appeal too, but I can't make up anybody else's face as good as I can make up my own. Valentino? He can take an old, beat-up lookin' hen and have her leavin' this counter a swan!"

I laughed.

"I ain't lyin'. You watch him sometime. He's just temperamental. That's his problem. Thinks he's a star and tired of waitin' for his big break. So he's cranky. And downright mean sometimes. That's what happens when you think the world is overlookin' your talent, I suppose. You start getting mean to everybody else you think got talent too. Now, see, that's not me. I know what I can do and what I can't. And I'll get mine. I know it." She flicked her hair, and I wondered what it was she wanted in her life.

A customer came, and Lissette said a big "Hi" to her like she'd known her for forever. "We were just talking about you. That's our new makeup artist, Carlos. He was saying, 'That woman has the kinda face I would love to work with.' And he doesn't say that often."

I knew my cue. Lissette was trying to get me started, have me get my feet wet. And I was dying to jump in.

"You do have a beautiful face," I said, "and your eyes are gorgeous! Do you have a minute so I could show you a way that you could bring them out more? As a matter of fact, if you started from the very beginning, even before you put on any of your makeup…"

When Rosalia came into my room that Sunday morning, I was busy making notes about all the stuff I could say to get
5 people to buy FeatureFace. It wasn't that hard, really, but I wanted to get to the point where I sounded experienced even if I wasn't.

"Yo, Carlos." I hated when Rosalia called me by using "Yo," and she knew it. "Why do you have to sound like
10 gangsta girl?" I'd ask her. But I guessed as long as she had Danny for a boyfriend, that's how she was gonna sound.

When I looked up at her, I couldn't move. I couldn't say anything. I could only stare.

"You gotta help me fix this."
15 "Fix it? I'm not a doctor. Are you crazy?"

"Why you getting so loud, Carlos? It's not what you think."

"Yeah, right. Your eye is all black and blue and yellow, and you're gonna tell me it's not what I think. Don't even
20 start your lie, 'cause I don't wanna hear it. You wanna lie, you should try it on Ma. See if she doesn't call the cops on that pig!" Now I really was yelling, and I didn't care.

But Rosalia was louder. "And I'm telling you, you're wrong! You think you know everything, but you're
25 wrong!"

I couldn't believe she thought I was that stupid, that I would look at her eye and believe for one minute anything but what I did.

"Now, if you would calm down for one second, I will tell you what happened. And, you know what? I don't care after that if you believe me. Do you think I'm that stupid to be with somebody who would give me a black eye?"

"Rosalia, you're crazy," I told her. "You can tell me anything you want to, but you're crazy if you think I believe you."

"Look, I'm telling you the truth. It's after my shift. We're all standin' around in the kitchen, goofin' around. I'm actin' like a nut and I'm showing them how I can cook, and I start pretending I can flip things with the skillet. And the freakin' thing is heavy, but I'm tossin' it around, and I throw it up and I'm supposed to catch it, but the corner comes down and hits me right in the eye. And I swear, I thought it knocked me unconscious. I saw stars!" I stared at my sister, trying to figure out if she's that good an actress, 'cause I'd certainly never seen it before. But she seemed to totally believe what she said, and she seemed to think it was funny even. I didn't say anything.

"And then I woke up this morning and I saw it! I totally understand how you could think what you did, and besides, you don't like Danny anyway—"

"No," I cut her off, "it's not about me liking Danny or not." What I really wanted to say was, "It's about me knowing that Danny's not above giving you a black eye. He's already attacked me."

But I didn't say it. Danny was capable of being violent for no reason except that the person was there in front of

57

him. But him hitting me doesn't even compare with him giving Rosalia a black eye.

"Rosalia, don't tell me anything else, please. You tell that to Ma. Has Ma seen it?"

5 "No, she hasn't seen it. Which is why I'm asking you to fix it, put some makeup on it so no one can see it."

"*You* put some makeup on it, Rosalia! You have your own makeup. Why am I gonna help you cover it up?"

"Because she's gonna think the same thing you do, 10 except she'll go crazy and she'll probably call the police on Danny."

"I hope you know that if he hit you once, he'll hit you again. You want two black eyes, Rosalia?"

"I'm not gonna tell you again, he did not hit me. Now, 15 are you gonna help me or not?"

I thought for a minute. *Why wouldn't I help her? She's my sister. It's the least I can do. But it's also telling her I'll do it again. And I won't.*

"I'm sorry, Ro. I can't. You wanna cover it up, you 20 figure out how. I'm not gonna help you cover it up."

Rosalia stared at me. I couldn't even look back at her. I kept thinking that Danny attacked two people in my family—me *and* my sister—and what was I doing about it? How big a coward was I?

25 Pretty big, I guess. I left before Ma came home. I didn't want to know if she'd be able to tell what had happened, but I didn't see how she could miss it. And I knew the skillet story would be pure bull to her.

I was so upset, I called Angie and told her to meet me 30 for pancakes. I eat pancakes when I'm upset. Pancakes with butter. And sausage and bacon. And syrup. Lots of syrup.

CHAPTER 12

I want to be perfectly honest about this, even if it's a little humiliating. Angie is the only one who really knows, and she's sworn to secrecy. For whatever that's worth.

Our code for it is "vegan," which we thought was hysterically funny when we first made it up. I'm a "vegan." What that really means is that I'm a virgin. I've never had a relationship, never had… like I said, I'm a "vegan." I've had crushes on people, lots of them. Usually they're guys in magazines or on television. Sometimes just somebody I've passed on the street.

But Gleason Kraft was the first guy to make me think seriously about how anybody who wants to get married should be able to. At first I was only daydreaming about going to Gleason's photography opening. But then I started to think about those articles in decorating magazines I'd seen, where Barry and Sid live in a town house in SoHo and Barry has a photography studio on the third floor. And Sid believes that no matter how busy he is with doing makeup for movies and television, it's important to be at home when the kids come home from school.

The reality was, we said hi to each other in the halls at school, and when I got up the courage, I yelled out pitiful things like "Can't wait for the opening" and "I guess you must be getting nervous 'cause it's getting so close." But Gleason never said more than "Yeah" and "Naw, I'm okay."

"True," Angie said, and laughed, "it is pretty obvious you more than like the guy, but I don't think he has a clue."

"Why? Because he'd never think that way about me? Or because he isn't gay and he wouldn't think that way about any guy?"

"I hate to tell ya," Angie said, "but I don't think he is. I think with Gleason it's all about the music. Just like with you it's all about the makeup."

"But that's the point," I told her. "It *used* to be all about the makeup. Now it's about the makeup and the guy."

Just when I was feeling my most hopeless, I'd laugh. "Well, I'm not giving up. It ain't my naytcha!"

And Angie agreed, "No, hon, givin' up seriously ain't your naytcha!"

Of course, what even Angie didn't know was that I'd found this website online where you could order pretty inexpensive gold chains with charms or medallions or someone's initials. I was looking for an A for her birthday, because she'd lost one and she wanted another one. It wasn't exactly my kind of gift, but the price was definitely right. After Gleason told me about his opening, I was looking on the same site to see if there was something I could get him as a present, and I found this tiny, old-fashioned-looking camera that you could put on a chain. It was black, which was perfect for him, and I wasn't sure he'd ever wear it, but I thought it deserved votes for originality.

. . .

When I got back home, Rosalia wasn't there. Ma was, and she couldn't wait to start in on me.

"Did you see your sister?"

"Whadya mean?" I asked.

Ma was watching an old movie on television, or at least she had it on. She had a mug of coffee in her lap.

"Don't give me a hard time about this," she said. "Did you see her or didn't you?"

"Yes," I sighed. "I saw her."

"And you saw her eye?"

"Yeah." I still wasn't going to volunteer anything. I wanted to know exactly what her take on it was before I gave her any information I had.

"What did she tell you about it?" Ma was studying me closely.

"She said she was fooling around with a skillet at work and—"

"So she told you that same lie," Ma barked. "You didn't believe it, did you?"

I sat on the couch. "What do you want me to say, Ma? It was a weird story, but she swore up and down she didn't get hit or anything, so what could I say?" I was whining because I was so frustrated, having to lie about what I really felt and what I knew from my own experience.

"I will tell you what I told her. If she asks you if you think I'm serious, you tell her I am. I don't believe that stupid story about a frying pan. I don't believe it for a minute. But this is what I'm serious about, Carlos. If I find out that bastard Danny has put his hands on her, if I find out that he's hurt her, I will kill him myself." She hadn't even raised her voice, but I knew she meant every word she was saying. And what I was thinking was, *But it should be you, Carlos. It should be you defending your sister. Even if you didn't defend yourself.*

CHAPTER 13

"Ohmygod, she's baaack!" Lissette was beside herself. She looked like one of those little hula dolls you see in the back windows of cars, shaking and spinning with this ridiculous grin on her face.

5 The first Saturday I saw Shirlena Day, she had on high-top Keds and skin-tight jeans with huge rips in the knees, and a huge yellow sweater that mysteriously hung very low in the front but sat up in the back, so you couldn't miss that Ms. Day had a seriously gorgeous bootay.

10 Lissette tried to calm herself as Shirlena got closer, but she lost the battle. She started stuttering and stammering like her brain cells were leaking out of her ears. "Oh, MMMMisssDaaay!" she said in this high-pitched squeak.

I might have been embarrassed for her, but it was the 15 day I'd hoped would come. Lissette had told me that Shirlena came in occasionally, and I definitely had been praying for the occasion to get here.

"How are you?" I called to her before she could even get right up to the counter. I guess I made it sound like we 20 knew each other, and that's exactly what I was going for without being rude.

Of course, this is where my manager, the lovely Valentino, would have shoved me to the background so that he alone was standing in front of Shirlena, but because 25 he'd called in with some Valentino crap about waiting for a locksmith (spelled *h-a-n-g-o-v-e-r*), I got Shirlena all to myself.

"Hey there!" she called back. The sunglasses were already off and she was giving me a HUGE SHIRLENA DAY SMILE.

"I'm Carlos!" I pretty much shouted. "Carlos Duarte!"
5 My mouth practically hurt from the grin I was giving her. "At the risk of sounding scarily cheesy, I gotta tell you how much I love... that ring!" There! I got her. She sooooo expected me to say what everyone else says that she probably would have bet money on how that sentence
10 would end. I could see the surprise on her face. She held out her right hand and glanced at the roped pearls on her finger. "Me too!" she laughed. "I'm so glad I gave it to myself!"

Lissette was behind me like a big shadow. Before she
15 could start in and mess up the moment, I told Shirlena, "Maybe I shouldn't be saying this as a makeup artist, but your skin looks incredible without any." The part about her not having any makeup on was true. The "incredible" part wasn't. I could tell she had oily skin, which I knew
20 must be a problem, because she had to wear so much makeup on TV. And there were teeny bumps on her forehead and chin. They were barely noticeable, but I could see them.

"Actually, that's why I'm here," she said. "Whatever
25 they're using at the studio is making me break out, and I hate it. See." She pointed to her forehead. "And this," she said as she pointed to her chin. "Yesssss," I said, sounding like I was looking through a microscope. "It's very subtle, but I see them all right."

30 "I had a little fit at the studio," Shirlena whispered. "I don't want to be a pain about it, but it's *my* skin, not the makeup artist's! And I keep telling him, and he can't seem

to figure out anything to do about it. That other guy who works here, uh, Valentine—"

"Valentino," Lissette piped up. "He's not here right now, but he should be here later today, I guess."

5   "He's been so good at telling me what to use, I thought maybe he could help with this."

"We don't actually know when Valentino is coming in today," I said as carefully as I could, "but I'd be happy to help you if I can."

10   Just at that moment another customer came rushing up to the counter. Thank God, Lissette turned her attention toward her and left Shirlena and me alone.

I was thrilled. "What I'm thinking," I told her, "is that if we can duplicate what your makeup artist is using on the 15 show, we have a line that is completely hypoallergenic, so he or she—your makeup artist—should be able to use it on you without any reaction!"

"See! Great minds think alike!" And it was definitely not the Shirlena-smiles-for-the-fans smile she was giving 20 me. "I wasn't sure it could be done, but I thought it was worth a try. Anything to get rid of these bumps. They're driving me crazy! Christian, my makeup artist, is really talented, but a little lazy and a little temperamental. Not a good combination. I keep saying, 'We have to do something 25 about this, Christian!' and he keeps saying yes, and every week I break out all over again."

"Well, you know it's going to take some experimenting. What we'd have to do is get everything Christian uses now and see if we can replace it with a FeatureFace product. 30 I'm sure it can be done, but…" I stopped and took a breath. I couldn't believe what I was about to say. "I wish there was some way I could get my hands on whatever it is

Christian uses. Then I could just work out the replacements myself and he wouldn't have to do it."

"God, you're such a doll!" Shirlena chirped. "Like I told you, he's a little on the lazy side, so maybe I could take your card and give it to him. And he could get in touch with you."

"Absolutely! That would be *beyond excellent*!" Shirlena looked at me as if she thought my enthusiasm was a little overboard, but I didn't care. There was no way she could know how excited I was for this chance.

"Why don't you give me one of your cards?" she asked me again.

"Oh! Yes. My card." I didn't have any card. Lissette, who had served her customer, handed me a FeatureFace card.

"I'm getting a new batch printed up, but is this all right for now?" I asked Shirlena, taking the card from Lissette and handing it to her.

"Sure," Shirlena chuckled. "You got your number on here?"

"I will have," I said, feeling ridiculous, "in just a second!" I grabbed a pen and scribbled my name and cell number on the card. I was careful to spell my name Carrlos on the card. "I really want to help you with this, and I'm sure I can!" I was gushing.

Shirlena was gathering her bag and getting ready to go just as a group of girls was headed for her. "I'm going to give Christian your card for sure. He should call you this week. I don't want to do one more show wearing that stuff he already has. So, thanks, honey!" She was putting on her dark glasses and sending off signals to the approaching army that she was in a hurry.

"Don't worry," I called to her. "I know I can fix everything!" It sounded like I was willing to move in, scrub her floors, and handle her bills and all of her legal matters. I was only hoping it didn't sound pathetic and desperate. 'Cause what I felt was the opposite. If she only gave me a chance, or if Christian did, I knew I could come through for her. "Make sure he calls me!" I shouted as she was moving through the store with the girls shoving paper at her to get an autograph.

"Valentino is gonna kill you!" Lissette squealed.

"Why?" I answered innocently. "All I did was take care of the customer. Isn't that why he hired me?" Shirlena was not quite out of sight. I yelled across the store floor in her direction, "Don't forget it's Carrlos with two r's!"

I turned back to Lissette. "Like I said. Just taking care of the customer!"

CHAPTER 14

I was beginning to wonder why Gleason ever said he'd invite me to his show. Maybe he meant it when he said it, and then changed his mind because he saw how geeked-out I got about it. Or his friends saw him speak to me and gave him crap. I couldn't tell. All I knew was that days had gone by and it seemed like it was some kind of delusion.

Until the afternoon when I was on my way out of school and I got a call from him. He had my number from when he took my model makeup pictures, but I'd always been the one to get in touch with him.

"Yes," I answered, half expecting it would be somebody playing a cruel joke.

"Hey, it's Gleason." He sounded shy, but then he almost always sounded shy. "I wanted to know if you would look at something for me."

"Yeah… sure." Whatever it was, wherever it was, no matter what time it was, the answer would have been the same.

"Could you, uh, meet me at my locker? It's on the first floor."

"I remember." I knew very well where his locker was. It was next to the biology lab and I was halfway down the stairs by the time I got off my cell.

"Hey," I said, and it sounded about as casual as if I'd said, "I came as soon as I could get down the stairs. I've been waiting for a call, a letter, an e-mail, anything!"

"Hey," Gleason said. "I wanted to show you something. Get your opinion."

I was thinking, *Anything! Show me anything!*

Gleason took out what looked like pieces of paper wrapped in plastic. "I was thinking maybe you could tell me what would be the best mat to use for my photographs."

"Oh!" I was really surprised. I didn't know anything about mats. I wasn't sure I knew what they were.

Gleason pulled the pieces of paper out of the wrapping. "These are just the samples, of course. They can be wider or narrower or pretty much any color I want." I understood then that they were paper frames for the photographs. "I was thinking about black, 'cause I think that would be more dramatic. But maybe that's cheesy."

"What's cheesy about being dramatic?" I said, maybe a little too loudly. "Your photos are dramatic."

Gleason laughed. "Is that a good thing?"

"Sure. Black is perfect!" I told him.

"Do you want to see the other samples? I've got gray and white and off-white."

"You can show 'em to me if you want, but I'm pretty sure we made the right decision." Did I love saying "we" or what?

Gleason pulled out the other samples, and I examined them carefully. "Do you have any of the photographs with you, so I could make sure?"

"I have one of them," he said. He pulled a small portfolio out of his locker. "I'm still trying to decide how big I should have them printed."

"Are you kidding?" I said. "For your first show? Go as big as you can!"

Gleason smiled. "The bigger they are, the more expensive."

"Oh," I said, coming back down to earth. I'd immediately started to see the billboard-size photos I'd already imagined. "Well, as big as you can afford, then."

"You think they're that good for me to have them printed big?"

He pulled out of his portfolio a print that he'd taken of Rosalia. It was larger already than the one he had given me to take to Macy's. Immediately my eyes went to my sister's eyes. I remembered her saying when I was making them up, "The good thing about you is that you're gentle, Carlos. Nobody will complain that you're being too rough. I couldn't have anybody who was too rough doing anything to my eyes."

Now when I was looking into my sister's eyes in Gleason's photograph, I thought that somebody had been more than rough with her. Somebody had been an animal.

"I don't know if they're good enough to have them printed bigger than this," Gleason said quietly.

"I think they're great," I told him. "Really. Great."

"Cool." Gleason the rocker nodded. "Cool." He started to wrap up the mat samples.

I took a breath. "I wasn't sure you still wanted me to come to the show," I told him.

"Why not?" he asked, looking surprised.

"It's been a while since you first told me about it. I don't even know when it is." I was trying not to sound too anxious.

"This weekend," Gleason said casually. "Friday night." He added, "You're still coming, right?"

Again I worked hard on sounding as casual as possible. "Sure. How could I not be there?"

Then I dug into my bag and found the little camera that I'd ordered for him online. I held it out, laughing, although inside I was suddenly a twitching clump of nerves.

"I was going to give this to you at the opening," I said in this voice that wasn't quite mine, "but maybe it will inspire you while you're trying to arrange everything."

What made it truly horrifying was that he stood there without moving or saying anything for what seemed like ten minutes. He was frozen, looking down at the little plastic bag with the camera on a chain in it.

When he finally snapped out of it, I was ready to take it back and run. "Thanks, man," he said. "Really, thanks." He reached out and patted me lamely on the shoulder.

Thank God I'm good at pulling it together fast. "Hope everything works out with the mats," I told him and I was already moving away.

"Carlos!" he called, and I stopped. When I turned around, I was prepared for anything. He might give me back the camera, he might tell me not to come to the opening, anything.

"I'm glad you're coming to the opening. And you shouldn't have doubted me, man. How could I show those pictures and not have you there?"

CHAPTER 15

Now that I was sure I was going to Gleason's opening, I decided to ask Soraya to go with me as my date. We hadn't spoken since I returned the ruined Stella McCartneys.

I was pretty sure she was determined to hold a grudge, but I was just as determined to get my friend back. I wasn't going to let our relationship go down the toilet, even over a pair of designer boots.

The store was crowded when I got there, but Soraya saw me right away. She was standing up on her platform above the sales floor, busy with customers. When there was a slight break, I took the opportunity to say gently, "Do you think you have a few minutes? I really want to ask you something."

Soraya looked down at me from her perch next to the cash register. Her whole body was saying so. "You can see I'm busy, Carlos. What is it that you want?"

I just had to eat the attitude, swallow it whole, and know that it would be worth it in the end. "You remember Gleason Kraft, the kid who took my model pictures?"

"Yeah, I remember," Soraya said, and I knew I had
5 definitely started to pick at an unhealed wound.

"A gallery is showing his photography and he invited me to the opening—"

"And what, Carlos? *What?*" She was so loud, people were turning around to stare at us. But I pushed on. I was
10 there for a cause. I was on a sacred mission.

"And I'm here to ask you if you would please go with me."

It was obvious that Miss Soraya-Anna-Wintour-Girl was surprised. But she recovered quickly.

15 "You have nerve, Carlos, colossal nerve."

"I know, girl. So do you. Now, will you go with me?" I was trying to sound flip, like *Get over it, girl, so we can get back to being friends.*

Soraya stepped down off the platform. "Carlos, you
20 really don't get it, do you? You are so self-centered, so determined to get what you want when you want it, that you will say anything, do anything, and when you lie and the lie backfires, you want people to forget it happened. Because… because why? Because the whole world should
25 do whatever you want 'cause you won't grow up and take responsibility for what you do and say?"

By now people were *pretending* to shop, but I could tell they were listening to see what happened next.

"I've already said I was sorry, Soraya. And I am."

30 "Well, you know what? My boss is making *me* pay for the boots now, so I give him *my* money to pay for the boots you brought back ruined!"

71

I was shocked. I thought she might say no to going to the opening, but I wasn't prepared for all this drama. Soraya's eyes, hands, neck, and hips were all going in different directions at the same time. I reached into my bag for my wallet.

"If that's the first payment you're reaching for, it better be good!"

I couldn't believe her. "Soraya, why are you being like this? Is this really the end of our friendship because I made a mistake?"

"Don't give me that, Carlos. If it's the end of our friendship, it's because you said you could be trusted and you can't. Who needs a friend you can't trust? Not me!"

I realized I had three dollars in my wallet. It was definitely not the time to offer Soraya three dollars. It was also clear that some people around me were waiting to see what I was going to come up with. I quickly tucked the wallet back into my bag.

"I'll start my payments this week. I just don't have enough on me right now."

"I'll believe it when I see it, Carlos!" Soraya gave me one last horrible look, then got back on her platform.

I shook my head and sighed like I thought she was making some ridiculous, irrational mistake.

When I got outside, I walked until I was past the store windows, where people could see me. Then I stopped. What a fool, Carlos, I said to myself. *All because of those ridiculous boots. It's not as though you couldn't have done the same job on Rosalia's makeup without wearing shoes that weren't even yours. Do you really think they cared that you had on those stupid boots?* Oh, well. It was done now. Over. The only thing I could hope was that by the time I'd finished making my payments to Soraya, she'd decide to forgive me. If not, lesson learned. The next time I'd be wearing Stella McCartney boots, they'd be ones I owned.

CHAPTER 16

Gleason Kraft's opening was in a gallery on Mercer Street in SoHo. I knew Mercer Street really well because that's where the Marc Jacobs store was. I could never afford to buy anything there, but me and Angie had been lots of times to stare at the clothes, and so had me and Soraya.

The opening was from six to eleven on Friday night. From the time I got home from school on Friday, I started getting ready. I went to a nail salon near our apartment and got a manicure. I thought about how Gleason sometimes wore nail polish, but it was black and he could get away with it because of the rocker thing. Except I'm sure some people still made comments, but that's the way it was in our school. You could get away with anything. You just had to do it with confidence or they could make your life miserable, simply because a lot of them didn't *have* lives.

While the woman was doing one hand, I called Angie. "I know what you said about giving Gleason the camera charm, but I still think I shouldn't show up to the opening emptyhanded!"

When I told Angie about the camera charm, we'd almost gotten into a huge argument. She'd insisted I'd gone too far by giving Gleason a present.

So Angie said, "We've already gone through this and almost ruined our friendship. What are you going to get him now, a car?"

"Don't be a creep, Ange. I don't have money for any-
5 thing, really, but I know I can't just walk in and say hi without anything to give him. It will be humiliating."

Angie sighed. "Okay, Carlos. I'm tired of telling you to be careful with that boy. Do what you want."

"Okay," I said sharply. "Let's meet at the Eighth Street
10 subway and take the train down, like I said." I hung up thinking maybe I was sorry I'd invited her.

I went home, showered, and shampooed. The whole time I was thinking how much I hoped I would get some sign from Gleason at the opening that he liked me as much
15 as I knew he did.

Probably he'd be wearing all black. That was Gleason's signature look. Black and red. I didn't want to compete, so I decided on my antique white tuxedo shirt, to let him know what a special occasion I knew this was and also
20 because the tuxedo shirt made me look pretty incredible. I wore my burgundy smoking jacket, almost-skinny black jeans, and these stiletto-toed patent leathers with Cuban heels. I slicked my hair back, and finally I dusted my face ever so slightly with just enough color to make me look
25 what I called "sun-kissed."

Of course when Angie saw me, the first thing she said was, "I'm really surprised you think that's subtle, Carlos. You're a professional makeup artist. You look like you got caught in a blush storm!" Then she laughed hysterically.
30 She stopped when she saw how beyond unfunny I'd found it.

"I'm sorry, hon," she whispered. "I'm only trying to be a good friend and tell you the truth. I know you're trying to impress the boy, but you don't want to show up looking like RuPaul either, do you?"

5   "Yeah, Ange. RuPaul, huh? That's definitely not what I was going for. I don't know how I could have miscalculated so badly." I never, ever fix my makeup in public—I think it's tacky when anyone does. But I didn't want to walk into the gallery with the blush storm effect either, so I took 10 a little color off just to make sure.

When I went to a flower stand outside a little bodega and bought a dozen roses to give to Gleason, Angie kept her opinions to herself. I got a little card and wrote, "To a great guy who takes great pictures. From one of your 15 biggest admirers."

The gallery was on the first floor and we could see some people out on the sidewalk as we were coming down the block. It was an older crowd, definitely older than we were.

20   When we got inside, it was pretty crowded, mostly because the gallery was small and winding, like a tunnel with photos on the walls. I wasn't even looking at anybody else's work. I was only looking for Gleason.

Around a corner he was surrounded by rockers that 25 were our age. They weren't kids from school, which didn't surprise me. But to tell you the truth, I didn't really see them, either. It was like one of those movies where everything else goes blurry except the person you're looking at, who's in perfect focus.

30   Just like I'd guessed, Gleason had on all black. He was talking to a girl with cranberry-colored hair and green eye

shadow. It was clear from 180 feet away that Gleason could have been reciting the thirty-six most commonly used prepositions in alphabetical order and she would have been mesmerized. The other kids were looking at the photos and calling out things like, "Awesome" and "Sooo cool!" I stopped in my tracks, causing Angie to almost knock me over. Which, of course, immediately started her giggling.

But I kept staring at Gleason and the girl with cranberry hair. Now she was hugging him as though she was hanging from a tall building with no net under her. I couldn't see Gleason's face, but his arms were around her and he wasn't letting go. What if I was totally deluded?

Oh, well. Too late now. My heart was crumbling around the edges, but I kept walking toward them. At least I looked good, I thought.

As I got closer, Cranberryhead happened to turn her body so that Gleason could see me over her shoulder. It was unmistakable. His eyes brightened and he grinned at me. "Heeeeey!"

Cranberryhead immediately pulled away from him, but she wasn't letting go. Gleason had to give himself a little tug before he was free.

"You showed, man!" *Man?*

But he reached for me. It seemed to be in slow motion. I felt his arms go around me, and I was trying to stay on my feet. He actually stepped on my right foot, but I didn't dare move it or try to get my foot out from under his. I closed my eyes and could feel how skinny he was. I held on to his back and put my face against his hair. His shoulder was under my chin. *Can he feel me shaking? Does he think I'm scared or on drugs?* Either way, I didn't let go, even though I

knew all the roses were probably mashed together like peanut butter cups between us. In the background, there was music playing. I don't know what the actual song was, but, of course, what I heard was "Here Comes the Bride."
And I went for it. I kissed him. Yeah, on the cheek, but I kissed him. And I was glad I did it. I had no idea what Gleason thought about it, but he didn't throw me across the room, so I considered that a plus.

Then he said to Cranberryhead, "Gabs, this is Carlos. If it wasn't for him, there wouldn't be any model pictures."

"Yes. You've said that," Cranberryhead told him flatly.

But Gleason continued, grinning. "You were right, Carlos! They look so cool really big. And people keep asking me who the girls are and whether they're models or actresses or both."

I looked up at the photo of Rosalia smiling out at the room. *I have to bring her here to see herself this way,* I thought. How different she looked from the Rosalia I saw stuck behind that counter asking people if they wanted chips and salsa with their burritos. There was nothing wrong with what she did, I just wanted her to understand she could do so much more.

"*All* the photos look great," I told him. "Congratulations!" And I held the roses up.

He said "Whooaa" quietly and took them. "Thanks." Gleason didn't look at me. Instead he took a quick look in Cranberryhead's direction. Then he said, "And thanks for the advice about the mats. Black was definitely the way to go."

Not the reaction to the roses I wanted, but I was sure it was because he was shy and hadn't expected them. I just had to get used to the idea that Gleason wasn't someone

77

who was comfortable accepting presents. I was still happy I gave them to him.

Cranberryhead was suddenly looking very confused and unhappy. "Are you going to stand here all night in front of your photographs? The place isn't that big. It's not as though people can't find them. We should go to the bar and have a glass of wine."

"You two wanna go have a glass of wine with me and Gabs? You look really good, by the way," Gleason said to Angie.

I could tell by the look on Cranberryhead's face that that's not what she had in mind.

"You guys go ahead. I wanna stay here and look at these for a while," I said, gesturing toward the photos. Gleason gave me what I thought was a pretty weak smile as Cranberryhead dragged him away still holding on to the roses.

I pointed toward the two of them moving toward the bar. "What kinda person wants to be called Gabs?"

Angie laughed. "Why are you so evil? He has the roses, doesn't he?"

"I'm not evil at all. Don't you think it's about time I..."

"What? Actually had a relationship?" As close as we were, Angie and me had never talked directly about me having a relationship with anybody. Even though I had known her through at least five of her boyfriends, whether they were for two months or six, I'd never had any to talk about. I called people my boyfriends to get a laugh, as though she took for granted how far from the truth it was.

I wanted somebody I could daydream about living with, having the cute puppy with, the apartment, the house in the country, and the rings that had our secret messages engraved on the inside of the band. Dumb, huh? Well, to me it was *beyond romantic*. It was the only way I wanted to live my life.

But it was Angie who finally brought me thudding back to earth with, "Gleason doesn't seem to be in any hurry to come back here. Where do you think him and Gabs disappeared to?"

"The bar?" I said weakly.

"Then, I think we should go to the bar," Angie said firmly. "We've been standing here for years, and I'm bored. The pictures are great, but there are other people in this show and there are lots of cute guys in this gallery. So can we please move to the bar?"

We left Gleason's photographs and headed into the main room, where most of the people were. The music was louder there, and it was more full than it had been when we'd first come in. You couldn't really see who was at the bar from where we were standing, but it took me about two and a half seconds to look through the crowd and spot Gleason and *Gabs*. They had their backs to us, and Cranberryhead had her arm around Gleason's waist. The worst part of the picture was that Gabs was holding the roses I'd given to Gleason, and it couldn't have been because they were too heavy for him to carry.

Angie saw the same thing I did. She said, "What do you want to do?"

"Leave," I said.

Angie was quiet for a moment. Then she said something only Angie could have come up with. "Maybe he's allergic. And he didn't want to say anything because he didn't want to hurt your feelings."

"Excellent try, Ange. Can we go now, please?"

But I guess I didn't decide to leave fast enough, because that's when I looked over and saw Gleason *really* kissing Gabs.

"Damn," I whispered, and looked away.

5 "Oh, no," Angie said quietly. "Ohmygod."

We stood there for a minute in silence before she said, "Carlos, I'm sorry."

I faked a laugh. "Why? I'm the one who made up the freaking fairy tale. Nobody told *him* I wanted to marry
10 him."

Gabs and Gleason stopped kissing. As though she'd heard her name being called, Gabs looked back to where Angie and me were standing.

"Are you going to say anything to him?" Angie asked
15 me.

"Yeah," I said dramatically. "Adios."

I walked over to where Gleason and Gabs were, with Angie following me. Gleason lit up as though he was seeing me for the first time that night. "There you are!"

20 I wasn't about to go off into some dream world again. "Hi. We came to say we're leaving."

"You're kidding. You practically just got here!"

"No, we really have to go," I said, and Angie slipped her arm in mine for support.

25 "Here, I'll walk you out," Gleason said. "I'll be right back," he told Gabs.

"Good night," I managed to get out to Gleason's girlfriend, or friend or whatever. I glanced down at the roses in her hand and wished I could take them from her
30 and toss them into a garbage can on my way out. Gleason wasn't even pretending that he hadn't given her the flowers I'd brought for him.

When we got to the door, there was a thick knot of people. I turned to him to say good-bye again, but he put his hand on my back and pushed me through until he and Angie and me were all outside the gallery on the sidewalk.

5 Then suddenly he was hugging me, holding on tight. The minute he touched me, I was confused all over again.

"Just so you know," he said, not letting go of me, "the gallery owner just told me that the best decision I made was to include the shots of the girls." I swear I could feel
10 his breath on my ear. "And all I could think of was that it was because of you, Mr. Genius Guy."

"That's really… sweet." I laughed nervously, not understanding at all what was going on.

"I'm serious. You're the best!" Gleason backed away
15 and said to Angie and me, "See ya."

I stared at him, trying to make some sense of the whole thing. It was as though he and I had jumped into our own private movie for twenty seconds, then right back out into reality. I wanted to ask him, "Who are you, anyway?"

20 Somebody called him. As he was going back inside, the last thing I heard Gleason say was, "Hey, man!" to whoever had called him. He sounded like the rocker guy from school who I occasionally ran into in the hallways.

But he didn't sound at all like the same guy who'd just
25 held me. Maybe they were the same person, maybe they weren't. I'd thought I wanted to leave, but the second Gleason was gone, I missed him.

CHAPTER 17

"Carlos?"

"Yes, this is Carlos," I answered. What came out next at the other end sounded like "Christmas New Year."

"I'm sorry, who did you say this is?"

5 "Christian Newtier." The voice reminded me of Valentino's, but it belonged to Shirlena Day's makeup guy. He was already late for dinner. "You told Shirlena about the hypoallergenic makeup. Can you send it over tomorrow? I'll see if I can use any of it." And he hung up.

10 From the minute Christian Newtier hung up on me, I worried about how to get Shirlena the makeup she needed when I didn't know exactly *what* she needed or even how to get it to her. Christian didn't give me an address to have the makeup delivered to.

15 By the next morning I'd decided not to say anything to Valentino. If Christian called me back, I'd deal with it then. But I wasn't going to have Valentino take over the situation and come to Shirlena's rescue when the opportunity had come to me.

20 Of course, Lissette had already told him about Shirlena coming in. I was in class when the first call came. My pants started to vibrate, and I slid my phone out to check it. There it was:

Incoming Messages: (1) Valentino

25 Ugh! Usually I'd be ecstatic, because it meant extra work at the store. But this time I knew it was trouble. I called him back right after class.

"I understand Shirlena came into the store, and you worked with her. Lissette said you made some kind of deal with her—"

"I didn't make any deals, Valentino. She needed help and I tried to help her."

"Shirlena Day is *my* customer. I know everything about what she needs. What was it?"

I didn't want to tell him. Why did I have to turn over all my information to him? Because he was my boss, that's why.

"She said she's allergic to the makeup they're using on her for *Smokin' Friday Nights*. I said we had a hypoallergenic line and I'd be happy to work with her makeup guy for the show to see if we could substitute what they're using on her now."

"*You'd* be happy to work with him? That won't happen. I told you, Shirlena is my customer. She's bought thousands of dollars of FeatureFace from *me*! So what's next? Is Shirlena going to call you, or is the makeup artist?"

"The makeup artist. And he already did."

"He already did what?"

"Call me."

"He *did*? And when were you going to tell me?" By now he was practically screaming.

"I'm sorry, Valentino," I said, not feeling at all sorry. "The thing is, I still don't know what Shirlena needs. The makeup artist called and he asked for the hypoallergenic makeup to be sent over today—"

"Fine. Where does he want it sent?"

"I don't know."

"What do you mean you don't know? Didn't he give you an address?"

"No, Valentino, he *didn't*." I soooo didn't want to be having this conversation with him.

"Give me his number. I'll call him back and get the address."

5 "I don't have his number. Shirlena took my number and gave it to him." Actually, if I'd thought about it, I probably could have found Christian's number on my incoming calls, but all I could concentrate on was getting off the phone with him. "I don't have the number," I 10 repeated quietly.

"How convenient."

I waited for any other snarky comment. I had no choice. Then I realized he'd hung up on me.

At that moment, yes, I did think that the whole thing 15 with Shirlena had been one big joke on me that had exploded in my face. Valentino would fire me, and that would be the end of it. *Beyond tragic.* It sucked.

CHAPTER 18

"You're gonna look down your nose at your own sister now?" That's exactly what my mother accused me of.

20 "I'm not looking down my nose at Rosalia. I'm only saying that people have choices, and if Rosalia's choice is to be with that creep, Danny, nobody is chaining her to him."

"Yeah, well, you're not her mother."

25 "You're right, I'm not. But even if I was, Ma, I'd still say the same thing. She's made her choice. Nobody's forcing her to stay with him."

Besides, our apartment was not that big. I heard Rosalia the same as Ma did when she came in at night and cried until she fell asleep. I heard her and I knew Ma heard her. Believe me, I looked closely for bruises when I talked to
5 her. If I saw any, I knew I had to do something, even though I wasn't sure what. But as hard as it was to listen to her crying, if all the tears were about him cheating or generally being Mister Pigman, there wasn't anything I *could* do about that except try to get through to Rosalia
10 when she gave me half a chance. And that wasn't often.

Ma told me, "I was watching a show called *Stop in the Name of Love* with this psychologist named Dr. Sydney. She was talking about doing this thing called an intervention. What it means is that people who have friends or family
15 who are doing things like drinking themselves to death or eating and throwing up or *lettin' somebody beat the crap out of 'em* sit down with the person and they talk to 'em and tell 'em they have to change—or else."

"Ma, I know what an intervention is. But ganging up
20 on Rosalia about that idiot is not going to do anything but make Rosalia cry and get mad at both of us, and who needs either one?"

"Look, Carlos, you're supposed to be the man of the house. Can't you act like one for once in your life?"

25 It was like she hit me as hard as Danny could ever have hit Rosalia. I felt tears immediately fill my eyes. I couldn't look at her. I tried not to even think about what she meant. It was too confusing. It hurt too much. I took a second so my voice wouldn't come out weird, and I said, "What is it
30 exactly that you want me to do, Ma?"

I could tell she was sorry. When I finally got the guts to look at her, she looked like she had tears in her eyes too.

"I just don't want either one of you getting hurt. That's all."

"I know," I said quietly.

"I want us to sit down with her and tell her that if she breaks up with this guy it won't be the end of the world." She stopped for a second. Then she said, "But if she keeps going out with him and he puts another mark on her face, I'm gonna—"

"I know, Ma. You already said what you were gonna do." Is that what she meant by the man of the house? Was I supposed to keep threatening what I was gonna do to him for hitting my sister?

Of course I was. I knew it, and I felt ashamed and embarrassed and scared. What I also knew was that even when those guys had attacked me, I hadn't defended myself. How could I be expected to defend Rosalia?

So what was I going to do to help the situation? To be the *man* of the house my mother was asking me to be?

"So when do you want to have this intervention?" The only thing more horrifying would be trying to fight Danny and his thugs.

"I don't think we should wait. I think if she comes home tonight, we should talk to her."

"Ma, she never comes right home. And I have to get up early in the morning, and so do you."

Ma gave me one of her looks, but I wasn't sure what it meant. Then I figured out she was considering the options. "I'll tell you this," she said. "If she comes home and I hear her crying, we're doing it *tonight*. This is where it stops. Do I have your word, Carlos?"

Ma never asked for my word on anything. When she asked me to do something, I usually did it. I almost never resisted. This was the first time in a very long time. And I knew she was right that we had to try to do something even if I didn't think this intervention idea was the best solution.

5   "Yes, Ma. You have my word."

Ma stared at me for a minute. "It's the right thing," she said. "We're her family."

Yeah, and I thought, *We couldn't be more different. I guess I should be proud we're all as close as we are. There are kids in* 10 *school who never see their families and a few who don't know who they even are. So, I guess I'm lucky.*

I wondered if getting rich and famous would mean it would be easier to protect my sister. No, I decided. It wasn't the money that would have any effect. But would an 15 intervention at one in the morning?

CHAPTER 19

Rosalia came home right after work. I was in my room, and Ma was in the living room. I listened to see if Ma was gonna start in on Rosalia anyway, but she didn't. When Rosalia went right to her room and didn't make a sound, I 20 knew the intervention was canceled, thank God. Or at least postponed. Ma and me agreed, or at least she *made* me agree, that if we heard Rosalia coming in and crying again at all from now on, we'd still speak to her. So, all I could do was hope it didn't happen.

25   At around ten the next morning, I was at my locker whining to Angie about my whole career being destroyed by the Wicked Valentino when my cell rang. It was the

store number. "Hello," I said in the most innocent voice I could get out.

"Hi, honey. It's Lissette."

"Oh, hi, Lissette." Angie smiled, but I shook my head. It
5 still couldn't be anything great.

"Listen," Lissette said, "Valentino wanted me to call you. It's about this weekend."

What was he going to do, lay me off? Tell me they didn't need me till further notice? He couldn't. There were people
10 who came in on the weekends especially to see me. Mostly women, but even some guys. I had a following. And the bottom line was I made FeatureFace money.

"What about this weekend, Lissette?"

"Valentino was supposed to go out to Hollow Hills, New
15 Jersey, to do a special appearance, but he said he wants you to go instead."

Whew! It definitely wasn't as bad as I expected. I wasn't getting fired. I wasn't even getting "laid off." True, if I didn't know better, I might have been fooled by the whole
20 "guest appearance" thing. But ever since I'd worked for FeatureFace, Valentino had talked about how awful going to another store was, especially if it was outside the city. "You have to get up extra early to catch some train or bus or both to some cow patch in Long Island, just because
25 they're trying to boost sales. And you stand there while these families of thirteen come in, and you have to make up the mother, the grandmother, the daughter, and the auntie all the while knowing they're not going to buy an eyebrow pencil. And at the end of the day, you crawl to
30 the bus that takes you to the train, and you get home at midnight, but you're too tired to do anything, so what is it for? Nothing. It's punishment." So, if Valentino considered

this punishment, that's exactly what he was dishing out to me.

"Did you say *Hollow Hills*, New Jersey, Lissette?"

"Yes. That's where the store is." The whole time Angie was watching and listening, trying to figure out just how bad the situation was.

"Where is that, Lissette? I've never heard of it."

"Wait a minute, honey. I'll ask Valentino." *I can't believe what a creep he is that he won't even get on the phone and give me my punishment directly. He's probably standing right there next to her, grinning like a maniac.*

"I gotta go," Angie told me with a look of sympathy on her face. "Let me know what happens."

"I will, Ange," I said, even though I know she's only going to the snack machine to see what she's going to eat through her next class.

"Carlos, honey?" Lissette was back.

"I'm right here, Lissette."

"Valentino says you should call the store and get directions."

Now, no matter what I thought he was trying to do, I was starting to get annoyed. How much of an idiot was he going to be?

"They didn't give him the directions, Lissette?"

"He said you should call the store," she repeated.

"Okay. Well, you tell him thank you for me, Lissette. I'm so excited. Tell Valentino I said thank you for the opportunity."

"Okay, honey." I could tell she was relieved. She'd done her boss's dirty work and it had gone smoothly. "See you soon," I told her, hoping it was true.

"Bye, Carlos," she said, sounding sad. Why couldn't she have said "Yes" when I said "See you soon"? Did she know something I didn't know?

CHAPTER 20

Both Wednesday and Thursday nights, Rosalia came home by midnight, which meant she had to be coming straight home. I was relieved, and so was Ma. But I was also curious.

Friday afternoon I caught her just as she was leaving for her shift. "Rosalia," I said, trying to sound casual, "what's going on? You've been coming home so early."

"Yeah? You waiting up for me, Carlos?"

"No. I'm a light sleeper. You know that. I always wake up when you come home. So I look at the clock. I can tell you've been early."

"That's really spooky, Carlos. It sounds like you're trying to play Dad with me or something, and that is sooooo not like you."

"I'm not playing Dad, Rosalia. I was curious. I admit it."

"About what? You waiting for me to tell you I broke up with Danny? Is that it?"

I couldn't help myself. "Did you?"

Rosalia was putting on lipstick. I'd supplied her with enough testers and freebees to last her a lifetime.

"No."

"But you haven't been going out after work?"

Rosalia put on another coat of lip gloss, and I could see her hand was shaking.

90

"Look, Miss Busybody—"

"Don't go there, Ro," I told her. My rule was that nobody calls me Miss unless I give them permission and I don't give anybody permission to call me anything except
5 Carlos or Carrlos or great or fabulous or genius or beyond genius.

"All right!" She was still applying lip gloss. I wanted to snatch it from her. "Danny's not allowed back in Burrito Village because Miguel decided that it really was Danny
10 who stole some of the money—even though he's *wrong*—"

"Who's wrong? Danny or Miguel?" I wanted to see if she was so far gone that she actually believed Danny was innocent.

"Miguel, of course." She glared at me. "Why am I telling
15 you? Of course *you* believe Danny's some big thief. Why am I even saying anything to you about it?"

"You know what, Ro? I don't actually care if he stole the money or not. My concern is you. I asked you if you broke up, and you said no. So there's my answer."

20 "So you don't care if he's accused of something he didn't do and lost his job for it?"

"Not really. Rosalia, it's no surprise to you that I don't like Danny. I don't care if he stole or he didn't steal as long as you don't get accused of it."

25 "I'm sure that's next. Miguel has been treating me like crap ever since he fired Danny, and looking at me all suspicious like he thinks I really did help him steal, and I'm about two seconds away from quitting that dumb job!"

I glanced at the clock. "Well, if you're not going to quit
30 tonight, I suggest you get going. I'm going to the day care center, and I'm definitely late. Let's get out of here."

While we were walking to the door, I said, "It still doesn't explain why you're coming home so early. Is it because Danny doesn't have any money that you guys can't go out?" Which was probably not the case, because I knew with a guy like Danny, Rosalia probably paid for a lot of what they did anyway.

By that time we were outside the apartment, and I was locking the door. Rosalia made this big sigh and started for the stairs. "What?" I said.

"Why do you have to know everything, Carlos? Is this for you or for Ma? I bet it's for Ma."

"It's for me, Ro! Isn't it possible that I care enough to want to know how you're doing and that you're okay?"

"Fine," she said. And I knew the truth was finally on its way out. "Danny and I had a fight about the whole stealing thing and him getting fired, and he said he didn't have to explain anything to me, and..." Rosalia stopped herself because she was about to cry, and I had a feeling it was going to be big if she let it out.

We were halfway down the stairs when she stopped and said in a very low, quiet, calm voice—almost as though she was someone else talking, "He told me he didn't want to see me anymore. Which is bull, because I see him all the time. He makes sure of it. And he's always with some ugly, trampy girl... And that's the way it is."

Her eyes were full, but I knew she wouldn't let one tear drop. So I tried to match her calmness when I said, "I know you don't want me to say anything bad about him, so I won't. I don't understand why you care. I just want you to be all right." And then I added, "Safe."

"I'm safe, all right," she said, as though whatever she wasn't saying was more important than what she *was* saying. Danny wasn't close enough to her physically for her to be anything but safe. But she still hurt. And for that, I was sad for her.

CHAPTER 21

Getting to Macy's in Hollow Hills was like a trek through
5 the desert without water. Of course, I had to worry about being on time. I had to get up when most kids my age were just going to bed after a hard Friday night of partying. I gave my eyes and cheeks a little wake-up glow, courtesy of FeatureFace, so I wouldn't scare anybody at the store,
10 and threw on my biggest dark glasses.

I was first in line to get off the bus. I could see from the window that Macy's was already open, and I was in a big hurry to get there. It was 10:10, and officially I was supposed to be there at ten.

15 The first thing that I saw was a sign announcing FEATUREFACE IS PROUD TO WELCOME CELEBRITY GUEST MAKEUP ARTIST VALENTINO! I cringed. *Well, here goes,* I thought. I threw my shoulders back and hitched my bag up on my shoulder, which made me feel stronger and
20 more forceful, entering the store.

"Are you Valentino?" a really young woman asked, coming up to me.

"No. I spoke to someone on the phone, and thought I cleared that up. I'm Carlos Duarte. Valentino and I—"

25 "Oh, that's right," she said, "you're the substitute or the replacement or whatevah."

I rolled my eyes at her, and it happened so fast, I couldn't control it. But I hoped she didn't notice.

"I'm Nigeria. I'm the assistant manager in training. Ain't nobody here but us," she said. "The manager, Carrie,
5 is on vacation."

Nigeria started showing me the store, and no more than five minutes after she had finished, my first client came up to the counter.

She was about 104 years old, but you could tell she had
10 *beyond major* bucks. Then I went on to my next client, who I knew wasn't going to buy half as much as the first, but I was definitely doing what I was supposed to—attract business and sell, sell, sell. After her there was a family—a mother, her twenty-year-old daughter, and a cousin with
15 severe acne. More people were coming into the store by now. I was exhausted and ready to go home.

My cell rang, and when I looked to see who it was, I didn't recognize the number. I let it ring long enough for me to get to the back counter before answering it.

20 "Hello?"

"Carlos? Dear, it's Shirlena. Sweetie, I need you to do me a huge favor!"

. . .

I felt a bolt of lightning go through me when I heard her voice. "Sure!" I said without any hesitation. What
25 difference did it make? I would do anything Shirlena Day asked me to.

"You're a doll," she said. "But I want to tell you what it is, because if you can't do it, I'll understand completely and I promise I won't hold it against you."

Okay, so now I was convinced it was a practical joke. It was Angie, or Soraya, or somebody who knew about the Shirlena thing and knew that right now I had to be standing in the middle of Macy's in Hollow Hills, New Jersey. Where was the hidden camera?

"I'll do it," I laughed. "What is it?"

Shirlena laughed too. "I don't know what's gotten into Christian, my makeup guy, but he's been acting like a complete idiot ever since I told him I wanted you to help us figure out something to use on my face. He said he called you. Did he?"

"He did. And I would have sent over the makeup, but he didn't give me an address, so I was waiting for him to call me back."

"Well, the truth is, he came in once to do something, but he was in such a horrible mood that we had a fight and I… Let's just say, he is skating on very thin ice right now, and I don't even know if he'll show up for our taping on Monday night. So I was wondering if you could come by with the hypoallergenic makeup."

I thought she had to be kidding. But then it sunk in. *Come by?* "Did you say you wanted me to come by with it? Come by where?"

"The studio. When we tape. I figure if he shows, great. If he doesn't, if you can come early enough, there's another makeup person here who knows how to do my makeup, and you can give her the hypoallergenic stuff, and between the two of you, you can figure out how to mix it or substitute or whatever you have to do. Would you be willing to do that? They'll pay you, of course."

All right, so it wasn't a joke. I knew that already. It's just that it didn't feel like my life, either. My dream life, sure.

Absolutely. But my real life? Shirlena Day was calling me to ask if I could bring makeup to her studio and help another makeup artist figure out what to use on her for a national television show.

5 "Of course I'd be willing to do it. I've seen the show a hundred times"— All right, so I'd seen it maybe five times, but there was YouTube, wasn't there?—"so I know I could figure out how to replace the stuff that's giving you a reaction."

10 "Thanks, honey. Now, here's the address. You can come and play, and I'll tell Paulette, the other makeup artist, you'll be here."

I stood there writing down the address of the studio where *Smokin' Friday Nights* was taped. Actually, I was tap-
15 dancing, a combination of nerves and excitement. I heard Nigeria out front telling a customer that I'd be with her in a minute to do her makeup. She came back to the section of the counter where I was on the phone with Shirlena. "You got fans out there, Mr. Guest Artist. It don't matter
20 that Valentino isn't here. The word has gone all over the store that the FeatureFace guy is fabulous! And they're lining up. So you better get your butt out there."

I got off the phone, and every part of me was tingling. It kind of reminded me of when I was ten and got frostbite,
25 except the frostbite went from intense tingling to intense pain, and so far, this was only the tingling part. But I was already thinking that in order for the dream to reach *beyond miraculous*, I had to make sure everything went smoothly and professionally so there'd be no doubt in
30 Shirlena's mind that I was a *makeup genius*! Since it was already Saturday, and I was supposed to be at the studio on Monday, I had to go to the New York store on Sunday.

I had to pick up the whole line of FeatureFace hypoallergenic products, called FeatureFace Free-Zone, plus whatever other brushes or pencils I might need. That way, I could go to sleep Sunday night—fat chance—knowing I had everything I needed for Monday at the studio. I didn't even have to shop for something new, because I already had the perfect outfit picked out. I'd wear my almost-skinny black jeans, purple T-shirt, and my black YSL sport jacket from Soraya's sale box last year. Oh, and my black stone crucifix for sure. One, it was the *only* accessory for every important occasion, and two, if there was ever a time to have a crucifix around my neck for protection and good spirits, it would be Monday night.

I went back out to the front of the counter, where Nigeria was making excuses for me. Another girl had shown up late for work, so she was handling some of the sales, but what Nigeria had said was true. The word had spread that this guy at the FeatureFace counter was doing makeup and it was fabulous. So the line never stopped until it was six o'clock and the store closed.

After I packed, Nigeria and I exchanged numbers and hugged. I stood at the bus stop and watched Nigeria as she got into her little green car.

"Hey, Carlos, man, you wanna hang out with me for a little while before you go home? I'll drive you to the bus stop after."

Any other time I would have said yes. But Shirlena's voice was in my head, and I couldn't wait to get back to the city to figure out what I needed for Monday and the studio taping.

"All right, then, Boo. Later. Remember Nigeria!" She drove off, waving and blasting her speakers.

If I'd known what was waiting for me at home, I might have decided to stay in New Jersey, hanging out with Nigeria. But to tell you the truth, I know now I could only have put it off for so long.

CHAPTER 22

5   "You tell your brother that lie and see if he believes you!" As soon as she heard my key in the door, Ma started to include me. I'd heard her from the time I started up the stairs to the sixth floor. She was screaming like the house was on fire, and to her the situation was worse than that.

10   "I'm not telling him nothing. I already told you, and if you don't believe me, then what sense does it make to keep saying it?"

"Because you're not telling the truth! And part of me says, 'Who cares what she says? Just go do what you have 15 to do. Go make that guy look as bad as your daughter looks. Only worse!'"

That's what I walked into. The whole apartment felt like a war zone. Ma was in the living room, and Rosalia was in her bedroom.

20   "You go in there and take a look at her and see if she tells you the same lie she told me!"

"What's going on?" I asked Ma, even though I knew. I really did not want to be in the middle of this. I wanted to take my phone, go back outside to Dunkin' Donuts, buy a 25 cup of tea, and sit in peace, making out my list of all the stuff I needed for Monday.

"You go take a look at her and you ask *her* what's going on."

Okay. I knew better than to press it with Ma. So I went to Rosalia's door and knocked. "Hey. What's going on?"

5 "Nothing. Leave me alone."

Ma was right behind me. She called in to Rosalia, "Open the door, Rosalia, and let your brother see what that bastard did to you. I'm gonna kill him. I swear I'm gonna kill him!"

10 "Ro, what happened? Did he hurt you?"

"I told Ma and she won't believe me. Stupid Miguel was mopping the floor, and I was running around like crazy because we were so busy, and I slipped and fell. I hit my face on the corner of the stove and I got a little mark on 15 my cheek, and now Ma's going crazy saying it was Danny."

"Let your brother see your face, Rosalia! Open the door and let him see it."

"No!" Rosalia yelled back. "I wish you'd stop. I told you I don't even see Danny anymore. He's going out with 20 somebody else. I told you that."

"I don't believe you," Ma said, still shouting to the closed door. "I don't believe you for one second. And if you don't open the door right now, I'm going to find that piece of crap and tell him if he wants to beat on a woman, 25 I dare him to try it with *me*!"

Ma left Rosalia's door and started walking toward the apartment door. Immediately Rosalia opened her door. I stared at her cheek. It was red and bruised badly.

"Please. Rosalia, tell me the truth. Did he do that to 30 you?" I knew what I wanted her to answer, even though I also knew I wouldn't believe her.

"I swear. I swear it wasn't Danny. I haven't seen him in weeks. He doesn't come around, he doesn't call me, I haven't seen him. He didn't touch me."

By now Ma was back. "Why do you lie for him? Why don't you tell the truth?" She turned to me, "Carlos, you look at her face. You tell me. Do you believe this stupid story about slipping on the floor and hitting the stove?"

I took a deep breath. No, I didn't believe for a second that Rosalia hit her face on a stove at work. But I didn't want to tell Ma what I believed, because I knew she was ready to go into the streets and try to find Danny. So no, I wasn't going to stand there and throw gasoline on the fire by saying, "Ma, you're right. It looks like Danny hit Rosalia, no matter what she says."

Instead I thought hard and fast. And what I came up with was, "Ma, I have to talk to you."

Ma and Rosalia both looked surprised. "What do you mean you have to talk to me?" Ma said.

"I have to speak to you. Please." I said it as forcefully as I could.

Ma looked at me for a second. Then she looked at Rosalia. In the moment of silence I knew I had a chance to do what I wanted even though I hadn't thought it completely through.

"Come here." I turned and walked toward the kitchen. Ma slowly followed.

When I got there, I turned to her and looked into her eyes.

"Ma," I said, just above a whisper, "please. I want you to do something for me."

"What are you talking about?" she asked me. She was still upset, but her voice was almost as low as mine.

"I want you… to let me handle this."

"What are *you* going to do?"

"*Please*. Just trust me. If I don't take care of it, then… fine. But give me a chance."

Ma was still breathing fire. The only thing I had going for me was that I sounded like I knew what I was going to do, like I really had a plan.

"I don't know," she said. "I'm fed up with this. I'm telling you, Carlos, if I have to look at one more bruise, I don't care what they do to me, but he'll never put his hands on my daughter again, so help me!"

"I know, Ma! Don't you think I know? But you have to trust me. You have to!"

Ma stared at me. "All right. You fix it. But you better fix it good." She went to the kitchen window and stared out of it.

I went back to Rosalia's room. She was waiting at the door.

I pushed her into her room and shoved the door closed. I kept my voice even and as calm-sounding as I could.

"Why do you keep lying about this, Ro? Have you looked at your face? He's going to kill you!"

"I'm not lying and he's not going to kill me. Why do you and Ma keep saying that? Do you think I *would* let somebody hurt me and not do anything?"

I looked at her. I realized there wasn't any use. I looked at the bruise on her cheek, and I looked into her eyes and realized she was going to continue to lie. Why? I didn't know, but I did know she would, no matter what Ma or I said.

I knew I had to do something, but I wasn't sure what. I also knew I had to figure it out fast.

CHAPTER 23

I didn't sleep that night, and I couldn't wait to get up the next morning. I wanted to go over my list, which I'd done a thousand times during the night, and make sure I had everything I needed for the Shirlena Day taping. I also
5 couldn't get the picture of Rosalia's face out of my mind, with my mother screaming at her.

I got up, went over my list for the thirty-third time, showered, and dressed. Then I tried to figure out my biggest problem in the next few hours—how to tell
10 Valentino what I was going to do with Shirlena, and get his okay. He'd never be all right with it. So how could I get the makeup I needed out of the store for Monday if I had to get his permission to do it?

It was especially hard since Valentino *never* worked on
15 Sundays. And I didn't want to wait until Monday, because that was too close. If everything didn't go right, I'd have to try to reach Shirlena at the last minute and tell her so, and that would be *beyond humiliating*. So my plan was to go to the store and call Valentino from there with as much
20 confidence as I could fake. I'd sound as though I was so sure he'd be all right with me leaving the store with the makeup that it was only a formality that I even let him know.

Before I left the apartment, Ma cornered me. "You
25 remember what you said, Carlos, about this thing with your sister. I'm depending on you."

"Yeah, Ma. I remember." I left the house shaking. Rosalia. Ma. Valentino. I could only handle one thing at a time.

When I got to the store, Lissette had a thousand questions about the Hollow Hills Mall. So I filled her in on all the details, trying to be brief.

Then I got right down to business. "Now, listen, Lissette. I have to talk to you, and I'm hoping you're the friend I think you are, because if you aren't, I could be committing suicide."

"Oooo, hon, that's a lot for a Sunday morning," Lissette said, looking worried. "Even Valentino doesn't come in with that much drama this early on a Sunday morning."

"That's because Valentino doesn't ever come in on a Sunday morning. And he doesn't ever come in early at all. Seriously, Lissette, what I have to tell you is really important. Do you think you can handle it?"

Lissette flicked back her hair. "I don't know anything I *can't* handle. So what is it? What'sthematter?"

I started with what she already knew—that Shirlena had come in and talked to me about her makeup for *Smokin' Friday Nights* and we'd hit it off. Then I continued with the call from Christian, her makeup guy, and how he'd never followed up. Finally I told her how Shirlena had called me while I was working at Hollow Hills, and how she wanted me to work with her for the taping the next night.

"Oh, baby, baby, babeeeee!" she squealed. "I'm nobody's fool! I can see how talented you are, Carlos! And I could see how you and Shirlena got along!" She stopped and looked down at the floor, then back up at me. "The thing is, I don't see Valentino exactly telling you, 'Go on, take all the makeup you want and you go work on Shirlena's makeup, when that's what I been workin' my butt off for all these months.' That, I just don't see happening!"

"I know," I said. "Me either."

"Ooooweee, he's gonna be mad!" Lissette seemed to be enjoying this part almost too much. "He'll be so jealous!"

"Do you think he'll fire me?"

5 "How's he gonna fire you? You didn't do anything wrong. The most he could do is figure out some way to send your butt back to Hollow Hills Mall."

"It would be horrible if it was permanent, that's for sure. So I don't think I have any choice. I think I have to 10 call Valentino, tell him the truth, and take my chances."

Lissette shook her head slowly. "I think you should come up with something else. Even if he doesn't send you to a mall somewhere, he could make your life so miserable here, you'd hate it. Or, because you're part-time, he'd give 15 you the kinda hours that you'd have to quit. I've seen him do that before."

"So what do you suggest I do, Lissette? Call Shirlena and tell her, 'I'm sorry. I can't come and take the opportunity of a lifetime because I'm scared my boss will 20 be jealous and try to fire me?'"

"It's the truth, isn't it?" she squealed.

Both of us stood at the back counter looking at the floor as if we expected an answer to spell itself out on the carpet any second.

25 "I think…" Lissette said. "I think you have to take this opportunity. And maybe you have to take a risk at the same time."

"What does that mean?" I asked her, not really sure I was ready for what she had to say.

30 "I think you should see if there are enough samples to take what you need. That way you won't be taking actual stock. If there are enough, then you take them and you go

do Shirlena's makeup. If she likes it, you tell her to call Valentino and place a huge order, or have her show call and it won't matter. Valentino can take credit for the big sale, which you know he will, and if he gets the commission on it, he won't care how he got it. But in the meantime Shirlena will get to see how good you are!" Lissette took a deep breath and ran her hands over her breasts like they were the exclamation points to her sentence.

"I don't know," I said.

"What do you mean, you don't know? You gonna pass this up?"

"No, but I never pictured me taking anything without Valentino knowing."

"You don't have any choice," Lissette said. "You will never, ever get Valentino's permission, so you can either call Shirlena Day right now and make your apologies and tell her you can't come, or start packing makeup."

So I thought about it for a minute or two, and then I went to the drawer to get the samples. It took me less than three seconds to see that I'd never have enough. Crap! I knew I'd have to take the actual products to make sure I had what I needed. I took a deep breath and got a plastic shopping bag.

I think I was probably praying as I was packing. It certainly felt like stealing to me. Yes, I was using it for a customer. But no, the customer wasn't paying before the makeup left the store. Wait—

I pulled out my cell phone. Lissette said, "Are you really gonna call Valentino anyway? I'm telling you, it's a mistake."

"Shhhh." I told Lissette. When I heard Shirlena's voice message I was disappointed, but I went ahead anyway.

"Hi, Shirlena. This is Carlos. I'm here at Macy's and I'm packing everything up, and I wanted to ask you, if we—or if *you* like the way things look after I do your makeup for the show, can I make a record of what we use and the producers of your show can buy it? So then, in a way, it would be like I'm doing a consultation at the studio with our products, and then, just like you'd do in the store, you'd buy them. Except it wouldn't be you, it would be the producers of your show." I was babbling, but I managed to get it out. It was a way for me to feel that I wasn't about to steal a couple hundred dollars' worth of makeup. "When you get this message, could you call me right away? I'm bringing everything we need anyway, so you don't have to worry."

No, only *I* had to worry that she wouldn't get the message, and I'd think everything was all right until I'd used all the makeup on Monday and she told me, "No, I never agreed to any such thing." Could that actually happen? Yes, but it wouldn't. I had to have faith.

I clicked off and kept loading the bag with makeup. Lissette said, "I think that was pure genius, Carlos. I really do."

And I said, "Thanks. Let's hope she calls."

CHAPTER 24

I was on my way out of the store when my phone rang. I didn't even check to see who was calling. I answered hoping that it was Shirlena.

So it was a shock when I said "Hi" and a strange man's voice said "Hey" back.

"I'm sorry, who is this?"

"Hey, you don't know who this is?" And by then I did.

5 "Gleason?"

"Yeah, how are ya?"

I kept moving out of the store onto Seventh Avenue. "I'm okay. What'samatter?"

I heard a snorty laugh. "Nothing's the matter. I wanted
10 to ask you something."

I frowned. The last time I'd spent more than a few minutes with him was at his opening. He'd acted like two different people, and worse than that, within minutes after I'd given him a bouquet of roses, he'd given it to some girl
15 I'd never seen or heard about before. Or at least that's what it looked like.

So where was this "I wanted to ask you something" coming from?

"Sure, Gleason, what can I do for you?" I was purposely
20 sounding like I was still in the store behind the counter, except that I didn't even talk to clients like that.

"Do you have some time that we could... um... hang out?"

Hang out? If it had been any time before his opening,
25 *before* I saw him kissing Gabs Cranberryhead holding *my* bouquet of roses, I would have told him the next six months were free. But not now.

"Actually, I'm superbusy right now. At least today and tomorrow."

30 "Oh. I was thinking since it was Sunday, maybe you weren't so... I don't know... So you're busy all day, huh?"

107

"Kind of. What do you want to talk about? Is it important?"

"It's sort of important. But I guess it can wait," he said. "You say you're busy tomorrow, huh?" He sounded disappointed.

"Yeah, Gleason, tomorrow is very busy. I have school like you do, and then I have a job to do Monday night." God, it felt good to call it a job! "Could we talk on Tuesday? Or do you want to try to meet in school tomorrow?"

"No, not in school. Tuesday's cool. No problem."

"Are you sure?"

"Yeah, I'm sure."

"Should we pick a place now or do you want to figure it out tomorrow? Or you can text me if for some reason we don't see each other."

"Yeah," Gleason said. "I'll speak to ya or text ya tomorrow."

This is hysterical. Gleason Kraft is going to contact me tomorrow to meet on Tuesday after I told him I was too busy today and tomorrow. Insane. Am I conscious?

I clicked off and ran for the subway, picturing Gleason Kraft. *Beyond beautiful* Gleason Kraft. *Maybe he wants to do more pictures. Would I do them? Sure. I'd probably do anything for Gleason Kraft. Even if he does have an insufferable girlfriend with cranberry dyed hair.*

CHAPTER 25

Monday at school it was as though Gleason had never called. Yeah, he was with his friends, which he always

108

was. And, yeah, he was on the run, which he always was. But it was as though we hadn't made a date just hours before to meet the next day.

I didn't let it weird me out, though. I had only one thing on my mind—my date with Shirlena Day that night. After school I would go to the day care center. Being around the kids always helped me to focus when I had something important coming up.

When I left the center, I'd go home, change, grab my makeup bag, and take the subway uptown to the studio. It was midtown and, from the address, I knew it was way over on Eleventh Avenue. That meant I'd have to make sure to give myself enough time for a long walk after I got off the subway. I paced myself at school, which means I had this look on my face in class that said, *I'm listening, I really am. You don't even have to call on me. Just keep teaching and know that I'm listening.* And, of course, I wasn't hearing much of what anybody said.

When I got to the center, things were so crazy they weren't all that pleased that I was only going to be there for an hour. But the thing was, I'm so good with kids and the kids love me so much that even an hour is better than me calling in. And besides, I'm a hard worker.

Forget about staying in the moment, though. It usually worked, but not today. But it didn't matter too much if I was a little preoccupied. It wasn't like I was gonna drop one of the kids or something. I'd play with Serene, or change Tujami's diaper, or help Chrystal drink her juice, and the whole time I'd be applying makeup to Shirlena's face in my mind.

By the time I left, I was tingling with excitement. I still had to go home and get dressed—there was no way I was setting foot in a major television studio without looking fabu-fierce! I was going to give them, *I'm in the industry and I'm a pro, so don't even think about trying to mess with me!* Not that Shirlena would. I just wanted to tell anybody else who saw how young I was and doubted my talent to keep their distance!

On the way home to change, Ma called. I hadn't told her anything about me going to Metro Studios to do Shirlena's makeup. I didn't tell Rosalia, either, so nobody in my family knew.

"Hey, Ma," I answered rushing into our apartment building.

"You didn't see I tried to call you before? Why didn't you call me back?"

"I'm sorry, Ma. You know I always turn my phone off at work. And I just got out, so no, I didn't see it. What's the matter?"

"What's the matter? I keep thinking about this mess with Rosalia, and I wanna know if you've done anything yet, Carlos."

I was running up the stairs, wishing I could have this conversation anytime but now. "I know it's important, Ma."

"So did you do anything? Did you see that piece of crap who's hurting your sister?"

"No, Ma, I haven't seen him yet. But you promised to let me handle it. And I will. But I still go to school and I still work and I'm sorry I didn't do it yet, but I will. Can you trust me, please!"

"All right, Carlos. But I'm telling you right now, I'm not gonna see her hurt and listen to her lie about it and not do anything!"

"I know, Ma, and neither am I."

Then, of course, she hung up without a "good-bye" or anything. What I wished for was, "Good luck tonight," but I knew that wasn't possible. How could she say that if she didn't know what I was doing?

The whole time I was at home getting dressed, I thought about my conversation with Ma about Rosalia and Danny.

I didn't even try to focus on the night ahead of me. I got dressed and did my hair and packed my bag and even checked myself in the mirror fifty times, all the while hearing Ma's voice in my head. "I'm not gonna see her hurt and listen to her lie about it and not do anything!"

It's not like I wasn't going to do anything about it. I just didn't know what. Or how. Or when. Did that make me an uncaring brother? I wasn't sure. And that made me ashamed. I had to do something. Fast.

CHAPTER 26

Metro Studios was so far west, I expected to see covered wagons. I'm not even sure I'd ever been that far over on the west side of the city.

When I got about a block away, I started to shake. I laughed at myself. Even though I was really nervous, I was excited. I was a half hour early. It was five o'clock, and Shirlena said she didn't need me until five thirty, but since when was being early a bad thing?

Getting into the studio was easier than I'd expected. Shirlena had left my name on a list, and I showed my picture ID from Macy's to the guard. After he checked my name, I signed in and took the elevator up to the studio.

5 The *Smokin' Friday Nights* studio was on the third floor. When I got off the elevator, it looked like I'd walked into a huge auditorium. It was pretty dark, and there were men setting up stage lights at the front. When one of the few women passed by me, I asked like Shirlena had told me to,

10 "Do you know where Shirlena Day's dressing room is, please?"

"Yeah. All the dressing rooms are back there down the hallway." She pointed. "And Shirlena's is about third or fourth on the right, I think."

15 I walked in the dark in the direction that she'd pointed in, and when I got to the area where the dressing rooms were, I stopped and looked back at where the audience would be. *Yep, I'm really here.*

I walked down the hallway, expecting to see stars on

20 the dressing room doors, I guess, but there weren't any. Instead there were either old, fun movie posters or posters of CD covers on them. One had a *Star Wars* poster on it and another had a *Saturday Night Fever* poster on it. When I got to the third dressing room on the right, it had an old Aretha

25 Franklin album cover on it, and I guessed it was Shirlena's, but I wasn't completely sure. Eventually, after I'd gone up and down the hall a couple of times, I saw a guy with a couple of dresses on a clothes rack use a key to get into the dressing room with the Aretha Franklin cover on it. I

30 waited until he came out.

"Excuse me. I was looking for Shirlena Day's dressing room. Is that it?"

"That's it, but nobody's home," the guy told me. "She'll probably be here in maybe a half hour."

"Thanks." I watched him move down the hallway, stopping in a couple of other dressing rooms, dropping off what were probably costumes. I was trying to figure out where to wait. I didn't want to go back downstairs and stand outside. But what would I do for a half hour?

I ran toward the last dressing room I'd seen the guy go into. When he came out, I said, "I was supposed to meet Shirlena here, but I'm early. Do you know if there's anywhere I could wait?"

"You could go to the cafeteria. Ya just keep going this way and turn to the left. You'll see it."

"Thanks a lot." When I got to what the guy had called the cafeteria, I was expecting to see what we had at school. But this was a pretty small room that looked like a waiting room with chairs and leather couches and a little area where a man stood behind a counter and heated food in a microwave for people. Nobody seemed to be paying for anything, except when they used the vending machines. I took out some quarters and got a soda.

I opened my bag and started going through it, checking what I'd brought against my list.

At twenty after five I couldn't sit there any longer. I got up and went back down the hall to Shirlena's dressing room. The door was partially open, and I could hear her in there singing. I knocked and called in at the same time, "Shirlena?"

She opened the door smiling. "I was just going to come look for you. There was a rumor there was a man looking for me, and I know where my seventeen boyfriends are, so I thought it must be you. Did you get here early?"

"A little, but I went into the cafeteria and had a soda."

"Sorry if I kept you waiting. I thought you might show up a couple of minutes early, but didn't I say five thirty?"

"Oh, you did. I guess I just wanted to make sure I got here on time, since I didn't know exactly where I was going."

Shirlena smiled. "I'm so used to Christian being late."

Exactly as Shirlena was saying it, a voice behind us snapped, "Well, he's here on time tonight."

I knew it had to be Christian. He was very, very blond with superlong black eyelashes and huge blue eyes. He looked like he spent most of his time either working out or at a tanning center, or maybe someplace where he could do both at the same time.

"I didn't know whether you were coming in or not, Christian," Shirlena said to him, sitting on a tiny couch against the dressing room wall.

"Why wouldn't I come? We're shooting tonight, aren't we?" Christian's tone was definitely *not* friendly.

And apparently Shirlena was *not* having it. "Carlos, would you mind waiting outside for a moment? I would like to speak to Christian in private."

"Of course," I said, pulling the door shut behind me.

It was barely closed before I heard, "I can't believe you. How dare you come in here speaking to me like that? And in front of a complete stranger? Not that it matters. You shouldn't be speaking to me like that at all. What exactly is your problem, Christian?"

"I don't have any problem, Shirlena. I thought maybe *you* had a problem. First there are all these rumors going around about how unhappy you are with me because you think I have a bad attitude—"

"You don't have to hear rumors, Christian. I've told you to your face. Your attitude is lousy. I told you that the damn makeup was making me break out, and instead of you trying to figure out how we could solve the problem, you gave me this song and dance about how makeup was makeup and there was nothing you could do about it and maybe I should see a skin specialist. And tonight you come in here with an attitude worse than ever—"

"How can you say I have an attitude when I came in on time?"

"That's not a favor, Christian. That's your job!"

"Well, how do I know I even have a job if I come in and that little boy is in here with his little makeup bag all ready to go?"

"You know I asked you to work with him after he agreed to help you find something—"

"I don't need an assistant, Shirlena! And if I did, it seems to me I should be the one to hire him, not you!"

"You know what? That's it! I came in here to work tonight, and you came in here to cause trouble, and I can't work with you tonight and I don't think I want to work with you again. So could you please leave!"

"Ex*cuse* me?"

"You heard me, Christian. I want you out of here. Now!"

I was shocked, but not so shocked that I didn't move as quickly as I could down the hall and away from Shirlena's door. I didn't make it that far. When Christian came out, I couldn't help but watch him. He slammed the door and walked past me without looking at me, but I could feel his energy.

I didn't know what to do next, so I stayed outside the dressing room. Seconds later Shirlena opened the door. "I'm sorry you had to hear that, and I'm sure you did. Are you all right?"

5 "Me?" I answered. "I'm fine. How are *you* doing?"

Shirlena laughed. "Are you kidding?" Then she motioned for me to come in. When I got inside, she closed the door. "I hate to say it, but I'm relieved. I hate bad vibes. They make it impossible to do good work. And that's what 10 we're here to do—work."

"Yes," I said energetically. But I was more shook up than I wanted her to know. I never expected to witness anything like that. I thought the whole thing would be one big joy-filled adventure. But it definitely hadn't started 15 out that way.

"Carlos, I've seen what you do, and I think you're great. The question is, do you think you can handle this tonight? I asked the other makeup people. If you don't think you can do it, one of them will just take over for the night. I 20 mean, we have a little time for you to try stuff out, and I know all the steps, so I'm not panicking or anything. But what do you think? Do you want to give it a try?"

I thought maybe I was back in the big joy-filled adventure, that's what I thought. "Absolutely," I told her. 25 "No problem at all!"

There was a big outline of Shirlena's face on her dressing room mirror, and she'd written down all of the steps so she could do them herself in an emergency. Once I knew what products Christian used, it was simple to substitute what 30 I'd already guessed would work.

When I'd finished, Shirlena took a long look in the mirror. I knew what I was seeing. But it was what she thought that counted.

"Fabulous!" She said. "And so far, no itching!"

5 Shirlena told me that after her first sketch, she would come offstage and I should be ready to help her do a ten-minute change into another role.

A few minutes later I heard a lot of applause coming from the studio, and Shirlena swept in like a thunderstorm.

10 "Hey, Mr. Carlos! Are we ready?"

I went into automatic. "We sure are."

"Great. First I get dressed. Then you have ten minutes to freshen me up!"

We were actually finished ahead of time. I realized I
15 was holding my breath.

Shirlena was up on her feet and heading for the door. She was almost gone when she turned around and rushed toward me. She had so much energy, I almost ducked. But she kissed me on the cheek and said, "Thank you, Carlos.
20 You did great!" And then she ran out into the hallway.

I sat on her little dressing room couch and stared around me. I was a high school student who had just done Shirlena Day's makeup for a TV show. I was one step closer to going from a kid wannabe to Carrlos Duarte, a famous makeup
25 artist. I looked up on the monitor and saw Shirlena's face. OMG! OMG! OMG! How could I get about seventy-five gazillion copies of this?

And that's when the call came.

CHAPTER 27

He'd only called me a couple of times before. Every time I knew that it was him, I took a deep breath before I answered.

"Hello?" I said quietly.

5 "What would make you think you could steal hundreds of dollars' worth of makeup from FeatureFace Cosmetics and get away with it?"

"I don't know what you're talking about, Valentino." My voice was shaking. Of course I knew what he was 10 talking about. It was my worst nightmare.

I'd left the message for Shirlena about buying all of the makeup, but we hadn't had time to talk about it, and now Valentino was already calling it stealing.

"Valentino, I just used the makeup on Shirlena Day for 15 *Smokin' Friday Nights*. I'm sure she's going to buy it."

"But she didn't buy it! Customers buy makeup *before* they leave the store, or they pay for it and it's sent to them. Company employees don't steal the makeup and then claim the customer bought it and will pay for it later."

20 "But she *will* pay for it—"

"Forget it, Carlos. You'll never work in this industry again! So I hope whatever you think you're doing with Shirlena Day works out, because when we press charges, you're going to need all the money you can get." And then 25 he was gone.

I put my phone on Shirlena's little dressing room couch and realized I was trembling again. I wasn't afraid. I was angry. I was angry that I was stupid enough to take the makeup out of the store and put myself in this position, and I was angry that Valentino was so jealous of me that he was twisting something like this to make it look like I was a thief, when all I was really trying to do was… Was what? I suppose it was to make myself look better, and it *was* true that I hadn't bought the makeup, so yes, it was stealing, wasn't it? Could I go to jail? No, I was too young. Wasn't I? But they could still send me to some kind of prison *somewhere*. God. Why was I so stupid?

I waited for Shirlena to come offstage. She came in laughing. "It was super! Do you think it had anything to do with the makeup?"

"I don't know," I said quietly.

"Well, I do," she said. "Honey, I have to change really quickly for the next sketch. Would you mind standing outside for just a second?"

"No, of course not," I told her, and got out of the dressing room as quickly as I could. I had to talk to her. I'd wait until after the show.

When she came rushing out, she said, "This is the last one. Wait for me. We gotta figure out how you get paid."

I hadn't even thought about getting paid. I'd been so crazy to do it, I would have done it three nights in a row before it hit me that people probably got paid a lot of money to do what I was doing. Didn't they? Maybe what I'd get paid would at least cover what I'd taken from the store. That way, Valentino wouldn't press charges and the worst that could happen is that I'd get fired.

When Shirlena came back into the dressing room, I bombarded her. I didn't want to, but I had to.

"Shirlena, I have to talk to you and it's really important."

Shirlena stared at me. "What happened? You just had a real success here! You should be proud of yourself."

"I am. It's just that…"

"It's just that what?"

"Shirlena, did you get my message about the makeup?"

"Your message about the—oh, yes! I did. I forgot! I can write you out a check for it and have the studio reimburse me. And please get some more. I think we're good because by now, usually with the other stuff, I'm already starting to itch and swell." Shirlena went to her purse and pulled out her checkbook. "How much was it?"

I told her I had to figure it out and I'd get back to her, but that wasn't the point.

"No? What is the point?"

"The point is, I took it out of the store before it was paid for, and now my boss, Valentino, is calling it theft and I'm probably going to get fired."

"You're kidding."

"I wish."

"I'll call him. That's all. I'll call him and tell him I told you I needed it and I was going to cover it. And I will."

"Thank you, Shirlena. I appreciate it. I really do." And I gave her a big fake grin.

Shirlena sat at her mirror and started to take off her makeup. It made me sad, as though it was symbolic or something. What I didn't want to tell her was that I was pretty sure no matter what she said, Valentino was still going to use it as an excuse to fire me. Even if he didn't press charges, I could definitely kiss my career with FeatureFace good-bye.

CHAPTER 28

Tuesday morning I wanted to wake up anyplace other than New York City. With a different name, different everything. Maybe it's because everything I wanted Carrlos Duarte to be was going to be ruined with FeatureFace firing me for stealing.

I wanted to think about what a success I'd had last night. Everything with Shirlena had been *beyond brilliant*, even though it had gotten off to a rocky start. For the next ten years I wanted to work with her on *Smokin' Friday Nights* and whatever else she wanted me to do. The feeling was incredible. I hadn't even graduated high school and I had done Shirlena Day's makeup on a superpopular TV show.

And the reality was, I couldn't tell my mother, because she wouldn't be interested. Because my sister was getting beaten up by her boyfriend, and all Ma could think about was murdering him. And I couldn't really consider it a success anyway, because I'd used makeup I'd stolen from the company, even though I didn't consider it stealing when I did it. And now I was going to get fired and I'd probably never get work in the makeup industry again. Nobody hires thieves, especially in department stores.

Of course there was the fantasy that Shirlena would hire me. But I was a high school student. How could she convince the producers of *Smokin' Friday Nights* to hire a kid who wasn't out of high school? No, my one night of fame and glamour was over.

I dragged myself to school. Angie knew from a glance that I had lots to fill her in on. But I couldn't even begin.

With Angie and me, it's either all the details or nothing. I told her, "I can't even begin to talk about it. All I can ask you is, if I was put in jail, would you come and visit?"

She said, "With a carrot cake every weekend." Then we kissed each other's cheeks and hugged. She whined, "Carlos!"

But I said, "I told you. Don't ask!"

I went to my locker, and there was a note stuck in it. I opened it and read:

> Hey Carlos dn't forget were suppozzed to meet.
> How abt. Tompkins sq pk.? I'll giv u a call. Gleas

I don't know how I did it, but I *had* forgotten. Believe it or not, the last thing I wanted to do was meet Gleason Kraft. Today was not the day. I felt like I was at a funeral for my life.

At the end of the day when I was in my last class, I got a call from him that I couldn't answer. When I got out of class, I saw that I had a voice mail.

"Hey, this is Gleas. I'll meet you in the park at the big circle after school at four. If you can't come, it's okay, but it's kind of important." Wonderful.

What was with this "Gleas" all of a sudden, and how could I not show up if he said it was important?

. . .

As soon as I got inside the park, I saw Gleason from a distance. Considering it was winter, it was really warm, and there he was in a short leather jacket and bright red tight corduroy jeans. If I wasn't so depressed, I would have probably been more excited about just looking at him sitting there.

He waved to me as though he'd been waiting.

"Hey, Gleas," I called, half teasing. I had to ask him what was up with that. It was obnoxious-sounding.

"Thanks for coming," he said, and gave me this big hug. He kind of bounced up and down in place like a marionette and then he landed on the bench.

"What's so important?" I asked, sitting down beside him. Not as close as I used to imagine sitting next to him one day, but there we were.

Gleason looked down at his black and red Keds. "You know... how I was so excited for you to come to my opening?"

Well, he'd seemed excited about having a show. And then he'd ditched me and Angie to go hang out at the bar with Cranberryhead and gave her *my* roses. But I said simply, "I remember that you were excited to have a show. And who wouldn't be?"

"No, Carlos. I was excited because we'd worked on those photographs together and now they were huge and they were hanging in a gallery and I wanted to... uh... share it with you."

Maybe it was because of the whole Valentino thing, I don't know, but Gleason Kraft was not having the same effect on me today that he usually had. "No, Gleason, I didn't really get all that. I was glad to be invited, though." Then I did something way out of character for me. I said to him, "Gleason, you said this was important, so I'm here. But I have some stuff on my mind that's really upsetting and important, so do you want to tell me what you wanted to talk about?"

I could see he was surprised. I didn't mean to be rude at all. But I *was* being selfish. I needed to think. Or I needed to call Shirlena and ask her if she'd had a chance to speak to Valentino. But I definitely didn't need to be sitting on a
5 park bench with Gleason chatting about his opening, which had already happened and which he'd pretty much ignored me at.

"I'm sorry you're upset about something. Is there anything I can do?"

10 "No," I told him. "And I don't want you to think you can't talk to me about whatever it is…"

"I guess I'm kind of stalling, because I know how stupid this is going to sound. I… I was talking to Gabs—uh Gabrielle… you remember her, right?"

15 "Yeah, Gleason, I couldn't possibly forget Gabs." I didn't mean to sound so snarky, but I wanted him to get whatever it was *out* already.

"Well, she was saying how she thought maybe I should have a talk with you."

20 I stared at him for a second. "Yeah? About what?"

"I've told her a lot about you."

It was like reading a mystery and wanting to skip to where you find out who the killer is. "You have? That's interesting. And?"

25 "So she knows how talented I think you are, and how much I owe you for asking me to do the model pictures in the first place."

"No, Gleason, you don't owe me anything. You took great pictures, and you got a show from them. The show
30 part had nothing to do with me."

"Okay. But I'm still grateful." And then we sat there, with him looking at the ground and me knowing he didn't make an appointment to tell me again that he was thankful I'd asked him to take some pictures.

"Gleason, what did Gabs think you should talk to me about?"

Gleason scrunched his whole body up like it had suddenly gotten colder when it hadn't. "She said… She said she could tell from the way you… were… around me, and the roses and the… camera necklace thing… that you probably had a crush on me, and that if I wanted us to have a real friendship, I should probably speak to you and get it out in the open. So you wouldn't be… hurt."

The camera necklace thing?

"I may be sick," I said quietly.

I didn't feel the least bit sick. What I felt was embarrassed and furious—with myself, Gleason, and the lovely Gabs—but I didn't want to show it or say it.

"Why?" Gleason was the one who looked like he was about to heave. "I'm so sorry. Maybe I shouldn't have said anything, but she kept asking me if I'd talked to you yet. She said I owed it to you as a friend."

"That was very kind of her, Gleason. Very considerate." I wanted to jump up and run, but I knew if I didn't fix things now with him, it would be harder—much harder—later on.

"She always teases me and says how people probably think I'm gay. She calls me Gleason Gaybait. She says I'm the kind of guy gay guys always fall for."

"That's hysterical," I said, thinking it was way past time for me to be rid of him. "Gaybait? Really, Gleason? Aren't you even embarrassed to repeat that?"

"I know it's stupid, but remember, *she* says it, not *me*."

"Gleason, it's late, and I have some important things to take care of. But before I leave"—and my voice was shaking because I was about to tell a very big lie—"I want you to know that I don't now and I never did have a crush on you. I didn't 'fall' for you like your girlfriend thought. I asked you to take some pictures. You did. They were good for you and they were good for me. I guess I made a big mistake by trying to show my appreciation. But in this case, Gabs's instincts are all wrong. I never thought about you as anything other than a kid in my school who takes excellent photographs." I got up dramatically from the bench, hoping like crazy that Gleason felt as foolish as I did. He jumped up also.

"I'm sorry if I said something wrong. I thought Gabs was crazy, but then she kept bringing it up—"

"Then maybe Gabs has the problem," I told him, smiling.

Now, of course, Gleason looked like I'd hurt his feelings by denying I had a crush on him—*make up your mind, guy!* "Is there anything I can do to help you with whatever you're upset about?" he asked.

"No. I should just go now, that's all."

"I'll walk with you. Is that all right?"

"Sure. Thanks." What I was telling myself was, *This was surreal!*

But another voice inside me answered, *No, Carlos. It was too real!*

Gleason and I were almost at the park entrance when I saw him. Part of me wanted to turn around and go somewhere until I could figure out exactly what to do. And part of me wanted to run up to him before he realized what was going on and start punching him as hard as I could.

But I didn't do either. When Danny and his slimy friend from Burrito Take-Out Village looked up at me from their bench with smirks on their faces, everything stopped. And for a second I didn't see anything but them. I didn't hear anything. I felt like I was totally alone. There they were, and I knew I had to do something that would somehow make a difference.

CHAPTER 29

"That your boyfriend, freak?" Danny called out to me. How ironic. I was used to it, but I expected Gleason would take off down the street and never look back.

I went right up to Danny. "You put your hands on my sister again, and I'll break your neck."

Danny got up from the bench and stood so close to me I could smell his foul liquored-up breath. Then he spat at me. It had barely splattered against my face when I saw his fist coming at me. As I fell back, I grabbed his shirt. I started to punch at him, throwing out my fists wildly just trying to reach his body. He smashed me between the eyes. I saw black spots. But I just kept swinging.

Then his friend came at me. I smelled both of them. I felt something against my head like rocks. I closed my eyes, but I kept punching. It was like being thrown into the ocean. You just keep punching the water.

Somewhere, from what seemed like really far away, I heard Gleason's voice scream, "Stop! Stop!" And other people were yelling too.

One of the two guys hit me so hard on the head, it felt like it had to be more than his fist, but I don't know. What I do know is that it hurt so much, I started to sink. I lost my balance and started to fall in slow motion. My face hit the pavement and my leg twisted under me. It felt like it was broken.

Then I felt someone pull my arm. It hurt so badly, but I couldn't pull back. Whoever it was let go of my arm and turned me over onto my back. I looked up at him. It was a cop.

"You all right?"

I couldn't say anything. It hurt too much. He put his hand under my head and lifted it off the ground. "Can you get up?"

I still couldn't answer right away. But I could see another cop holding on to Danny and his friend. They both stared at me, looking like they were hoping the cops would disappear so we could pick up where we left off. Closer to where I was, Gleason was also staring at me. His hands were covering his nose and mouth, and his face was covered in blood.

We looked at each other. I wanted to tell him I was sorry. It wasn't his fight. There was a small crowd standing there. The cop asked me again, "You think you can stand, or should we call an ambulance?"

"No," I heard myself say, but my ears were stopped up. "I can get up." The cop started to help me, and he said, "Somebody said these guys jumped you."

I looked at Danny and his friend. A woman called out, "They did! You need me as a witness, you got it! Those boys were on their way out of the park, and then one of these kids said something to 'em and before you know it, they was beatin' the livin' daylights out of 'em."

"That true?" the cop said to me.

I didn't say anything.

"If they did, you gotta say something. If you wanna fill out a report, we'll take all o' yas to the police station and you can fill out a report."

I looked at Danny. He wasn't afraid of anything. He was still sneering. I thought about Rosalia's face and the bruises and the nights I'd heard her in her room crying. And Ma saying to me, "Either you do something or I will."

"Yeah," I told the cop. "I want to do whatever I have to. They attacked me and my friend when we were leaving the park. And he also beat up my sister."

I told Gleason he didn't have to come with me, he didn't have to get involved. But he wanted to. The police station was a few blocks away. I'd passed it dozens of times, but never thought I'd be inside.

I don't know what will happen with it all. The cops said they couldn't do anything about Rosalia, and then they said from the story the guys told, it wasn't clear if we were attacked or if it was a fight because I was mad about what "allegedly" happened to my sister. To hear Danny tell it, Rosalia was mad because he broke up with her. He claimed she told me lies and then me and Gleason attacked him and his friend because of what she'd said.

But you know what? I'm glad I filled out the papers and I'm glad Danny heard me tell the cops what he'd done to Rosalia, because he knows he can't bully our family and get away with it. Because if it happens again, there will already be a record of it with the police. Seems to me that ought to mean *something*.

CHAPTER 30

━━━━━━━━━━

5 Gleason came home with me. At first he thought he had a broken nose, but it was only bleeding like crazy and swollen. A cop took a look at him at the police station and told him he should definitely have a doctor take a look at it, but that he didn't think it was broken. "That guy wasn't
10 a doctor, Gleason. You should go to the emergency room," I told him.

But he said, "I just wanna make sure you get home first. You're a lot worse-looking than I am."

"Thanks, Gleason. That's reassuring," I said, and I would
15 have laughed, except my whole face alternated between terrible pain and no feeling at all. The cops actually drove us to my apartment building, which was a first for me, and I hope the last. They offered to take Gleason home too, but he insisted on coming to my apartment.

20 When we got upstairs, Ma was there. She went crazy. She took one look at me and wanted to take us *both* to the emergency room. I hadn't really seen myself, but when I did, I was *beyond horrified*. I don't really consider myself vain, but pleeeease! You should have seen me. It was scary.

25 I explained to her in detail what happened, and of course she was furious that now Danny had bruised not one but two of her kids. "Ma, let it go until we see what

happens. At least I filled out the paperwork. If this guy does anything else to anybody, his name is on file. Now the thing is trying to convince Ro that he's not a sane choice for a boyfriend."

5 Ma was working on me and Gleason at the same time. Wet washcloths, ice, Bacitracin ointment. "I'm not a surgeon, ya know," she said to Gleason. "I don't wanna keep doin' stuff to your nose and then have you find out it's broken. Your parents will sue me." Gleason laughed
10 and promised they wouldn't.

I could tell she was really curious about him. She said to me in front of him, "You never mentioned Gleason to me. He's a good kid. And God knows, somebody who'll fight for you? That's more than a friend."

15 I told her loud and clear, "No, Ma, he's a good *friend*. Not *more* than a friend. A good *friend*." I hoped that satisfied Gleason. I didn't want him thinking he was "my hero" again, no matter what had happened in the park.

Ma even said she'd make dinner for us, but Gleason
20 said he had to get home, which made sense considering the shape he was in.

When he left, I went out to the hall to talk to him for a minute. I would have gone downstairs except it hurt too much, and Ma said if she heard me on the stairs, she'd
25 come get me and drag me back inside.

But I wanted to tell him thank you. And that I knew he didn't have to help me out there. He and I knew part of the reason for the fight was Rosalia, but part of it was because the pig brothers thought we were gay, and that
30 was enough to beat on us.

"I'm not gonna stay out here long," I told him in the hallway. "I don't wanna scare my mother, but I feel like

131

I'm *beyond dead*. So I'm gonna go in and go to bed. But I just wanna say I'm sooo sorry you got hurt, and thanks for not leaving me there."

"I wouldn't," Gleason said. "I haven't been in a freakin' fight since I was in fifth grade, but I wouldn't have left you there."

As he went down the stairs, I yelled to him, "Think about going to a doctor, just in case your nose is broken!"

And he yelled back up, "Sometimes guys with broken noses look really hot!"

Inside our apartment Ma was cleaning up the little emergency room she'd created. She said, "I didn't tell you to get yourself killed, Carlos. It's bad enough the guy was beatin' on your sister. I don't want him to kill the whole family."

"I didn't think about it, Ma. I guess I just kinda went crazy."

"Well, don't go so crazy that you get hurt. You're gonna be famous. You can't afford to get all scarred up."

I laughed. "I was bein' *manly*."

"I know," Ma laughed back. "Next time don't try so hard."

When I got into bed about twenty minutes later, I checked my phone for messages. Nothing. Nada. I decided that no matter what I felt like, I was skipping school the next day and going to Macy's. I was going to the Feature-Face counter and facing the Valentino dragon.

CHAPTER 31

I looked as good as I could, considering. I put on my Gucci dark glasses—the biggest I owned—to cover as much of the bruising as possible. Classic oxford black linen shirt, tapered dress pants, and Florsheims. I looked like a
5 fashionable priest going to beg for mercy.

A few feet from the counter, I saw Craig Denton. The same man who was practically responsible for hiring me. I turned around and went directly to the men's room. All I could think of was that Valentino had called him to come
10 from the main offices and talk about the scandal.

I was hyperventilating. I'd pictured trying to calm a screaming Valentino, but I'd never pictured Valentino smirking over Craig Denton's shoulder as they waited for me to be arrested and dragged through the store in
15 handcuffs.

Carlos! Caaaarrrrlllooos! Get yourself together! I stopped daydreaming and came out of the stall. I washed my hands, waited until two other people left the bathroom, and looked at myself without my dark glasses on. What a
20 horrible way to get arrested.

I slowly opened the door and walked what felt like five miles toward the counter. Lissette was there, waiting on a customer. She looked at me like I was arriving for my appointment with the electric chair. I mouthed "Hi" but
25 nothing came out.

In a second and a half, Craig came out, followed by Valentino.

"Mr. Duarte. We were just talking about you." He stared at my face. "What on earth happened to you?"

"I fell," I told him, and I immediately thought of Rosalia's lies. I didn't know what else to say, and what difference did it make to him anyway?

"Val, did you say there was a place where we could meet privately with Mr. Duarte?"

Okay, so Craig Denton was calling me Mr. Duarte, as though it may as well have been "the defendant," and I was sure whatever room they were taking me to would have at least one detective in it.

I took one last look at Lissette as Valentino led us to the elevator. She looked like whatever I was headed for was happening to her. I guess she really liked me, I thought sadly.

We went up to the twelfth floor, where the human resources offices were. When we passed the tenth floor, where Angie worked in the Linens department, I tried to picture her saying a prayer for me, even if she wasn't working that day.

Valentino led us into what looked more like a conference room. There was a long table with chairs around it. He still hadn't said anything to me.

Craig Denton told me, "Sit down, Carlos." I was grateful for the "Carlos" and that his tone sounded gentler. I sat, and so did they. Except they were across from me on the other side, like we were already in court.

"Let me get right to the point. Apparently you've done something pretty stupid."

I breathed in deeply, and kept looking at him.

"You could, as I understand it, be arrested for stealing from this company."

There was a second of silence before he asked, "Is that correct, Carlos?"

"I was hoping it would be considered borrowing stuff I needed until the customer could pay for it."

Valentino snorted.

"I mean, I was hoping that the customer was going to
buy it and then it wouldn't be considered stealing."

Valentino finally said something. "The point is, the products were carried out of the store—you carried them out of the store without paying for them. Isn't that right?"

"Yes," I said quietly.

"And that constitutes *theft*," Valentino said. It was true, but it was also true I could hear that Valentino was enjoying himself.

"And did you come back today to steal *more* products?"

"Of course not. I mean, no, I didn't. I came back to talk
to you about what happened."

"Carlos, you're a smart guy. With a lot of ambition," Craig said to me. "Don't you get that this could destroy any chance you might have at success in this business?"

"Yes, I do. Like you said, it was stupid. I wasn't thinking.
I didn't mean to do anything criminal. I'm sorry."

Right on cue Valentino snorted again.

"The only thing that saved you in this mess was the deal we made with *SFN*, thanks to Shirlena Day," Craig said. "We could still fire you and take you to court if we
wanted to. But I've decided to call what you did damned poor judgment instead of a criminal act. Shirlena called raving about what a genius job you did with her makeup for the show, and she said her producers were going to buy lots of everything you used on her. And, of course,
Valentino, being as smart as he is, asked if we could get some kind of credit, and the producers are getting back to

our marketing department to negotiate. So, it turns out, ultimately, to be a good situation for us."

By this time Valentino was smiling and stroking his hair. He looked like a cartoon lion.

5 "It doesn't erase what you did or the fact that I don't think you can be trusted," Valentino said with both eyebrows raised. "And I've told Craig that I personally don't want to work with someone I can't trust."

I swallowed hard. And even though I didn't especially 10 like Valentino, I had to respect his decision. I stood, ready to leave. "I understand. I know I made a huge mistake. I'm very sorry for any trouble I've caused you."

Craig Denton stood as well. "Carlos, the trouble you've caused, you've caused for yourself. I've asked Valentino to 15 give you a second chance."

I looked at Valentino. If he'd looked like he was happy to have so much power over what happened to me before, now he looked like he'd won the whole poker game. He leaned forward in my direction, but he wouldn't look at 20 me.

"I'm not one who's big on second chances. And I told Craig that I have very mixed feelings about this. But I've decided to"—and this is when he looked up at me—"put you on probation."

25 I wasn't sure I'd heard him right, but I didn't ask.

"From now until I decide otherwise, I'll be watching you like a hawk. One false move, and you're out."

"I understand. I do. Thank you."

Valentino got up slowly and dramatically. "Oh, don't 30 thank *me*. Not at all. If it weren't for Mr. Denton, you wouldn't have a prayer at FeatureFace, believe me."

We all walked to the door and got onto the elevator together. I'd just left my own funeral, and somehow I was still alive.

On the way down I could feel my phone vibrating. I didn't dare take it out.

When we got to the main floor, we walked to the FeatureFace counter. I didn't know exactly what to do, so I said, "Thank you again! I'll see you this weekend."

Craig smiled at me, and Valentino kept walking. It was not going to be easy.

A few feet away from the counter, I took out my phone.

There was a message from Rosalia. So I called her back. I would have put it off because I felt so shook up from the whole FeatureFace thing, but I knew she'd avoided me since Danny had beaten me up.

"Rosalia? What's up?"

There was a big silence. Then my sister said very quietly, "I'm sorry about what he did to you, Carlos." All I could think of was how many times "I'm sorry" had been said by someone in our family today. I'd said it about fifty times, and now Rosalia, who was definitely not a "sorry" girl at all, was apologizing to me for maybe the first time since we were toddlers.

"It's not so bad," I told her, laughing. "With plastic surgery I'll look almost the same."

"I feel horrible," she said.

"I feel horrible about what he did to you. I won't ask you if it's over." But I was hoping she'd tell me what I wanted to hear. When I didn't hear anything, I pretty much had my answer. Who knew what it would take to make her leave Danny?

After the silence Rosalia said, "I gotta go, hon."

And I said, "Okay. I guess I'll see you at home." Now all I could do was pray.

I called Shirlena's number. I wanted to leave a message saying thank you for what she'd said to the big boys at FeatureFace. I was surprised when she actually answered.

"Shirlena? This is Carlos."

"Hi, honey. I called your company."

"I know. I wanted to thank you."

"I think it went really well. I'm glad you called. We didn't talk about how you get paid for the show. And we didn't talk about next week. I know you go to school. How is that for you, coming in to do my makeup for the show? I'd love for you to come back, but I don't want to mess around with your school stuff."

"No." That's all I could get out.

"No? So you don't think you can do it?"

"No, I meant it's not interfering with my school stuff. I'm sure I can do it."

"I mean it, Carlos. I'd love to have you, but I don't want to be the cause of you not graduating or something."

"Oh, I promise. You wouldn't be. I mean, there's no problem. Really."

"Okay, then. Let me talk to the producer and let's see how it goes. All right, honey?"

"Yes, Shirlena. Sure."

"You're a talented guy, Carlos."

So I hung up with Shirlena and almost got run over crossing Thirty-fourth Street. I caught a glimpse of myself reflected in a store window. My head was swollen, my face was swollen. I looked like I was on a lunch break from filming a horror movie about tastefully dressed Hispanic high school monsters.

I didn't have a boyfriend—he was something I made up, and yeah, I was still a little embarrassed even though he proved he was a good friend.

And speaking of friends, I'd lost one of my best ones—Soraya-Anna-Wintour. The most I could do was hope with time and payments on the Stella McCartneys, she'd forgive me for being such a big liar.

I'd definitely have to prove myself to Valentino to keep my job.

My sister was crazy about a criminal who had beat me up and left me looking like a piece of dog meat.

But you know what? When I looked at my swollen, scratched-up face looking back at me in the store window reflection, I still saw Carrlos Duarte, makeup artist to the stars! And the rest, sooner or later, I'd figure out.

Abbreviations

sb. = somebody; sth. = something;

etw. = etwas; jmdm. = jemandem; jmdn. = jemanden;

Sing. = Singular; umg. = umgangssprachlich

A

account executive [ə'kaʊnt
ɪg'zekjətɪv] *hier:*
Regionalleiter(in)

(to) **accuse** [ə'kjuːz] anklagen;
beschuldigen

addict ['ædɪkt] Abhängige(r)

admirer [əd'maɪərə]
Bewunderer(-in)

(to) **admit** [əd'mɪt] zugeben

(to) **adore** [ə'dɔː] bewundern;
anbeten

(to) **afford** [ə'fɔːd] sich etw.
leisten

aisle [aɪl] Gang

allegedly [ə'ledʒɪdli] angeblich

(to) **alternate** ['ɔːltəneɪt]
(ab)wechseln

amount [ə'maʊnt] Menge

annoyed [ə'nɔɪd] verärgert

anxious ['æŋkʃəs] ungeduldig

(to) **apologize** [ə'pɒlədʒaɪz] sich
entschuldigen

appearance [ə'pɪərəns] Auftritt

application [ˌæplɪ'keɪʃn]
Bewerbung

(to) **apply** [ə'plaɪ] auftragen
(to) **apply for sth.** sich für etw.
bewerben

(to) **appreciate** [ə'priːʃieɪt] zu
schätzen wissen

armed [ɑːmd] bewaffnet

(to) **arrest** [ə'rest] verhaften

ashamed [ə'ʃeɪmd]: (to) **be
ashamed** sich schämen

ass [æs] *vulgär* Arsch

assault [ə'sɔːlt] Körperverletzung

attention [ə'tɛnʃn] Beachtung

attitude ['ætɪtjuːd] Einstellung

(to) **avoid** [ə'vɔɪd] meiden

B

(to) **babble** ['bæbl] brabbeln

backward ['bækwəd]
rückwärtsgewandt

barely ['beəli] kaum

basement ['beɪsmənt]
Untergeschoss

(to) **beg** [bɛg] anflehen
(to) **beg for mercy** um Gnade
bitten

belly ['beli] Bauch

bench [bentʃ] Bank

(to) **bet** [bet] wetten

beyond [bɪ'jɒnd] mehr als

bill [bɪl] Rechnung

billboard-size [ˌbɪlbɔːd'saɪz] riesig

(to) **bleed** [bliːd] bluten
bloody ['blʌdi] *umg.* verdammt
blush [blʌʃ] Rouge
blurry ['blɜːri] unscharf
bodega [boʊ'deɪɡə]
  Lebensmittelgeschäft
(to) **boil** [bɔɪl] kochen
bolt [bəʊlt]: **bolt of lightning** Blitz
(to) **boost** [buːst] steigern
bootay ['buːteɪ] *umg.* Po
booth [buːð] Sitzecke
bra [brɑː] BH
bracelet ['breɪslɪt] Armband
breast [brest] Brust
(to) **breathe** [briːð] atmen
bride [braɪd] Braut
(to) **brighten** ['braɪtn] aufleuchten
bruise [bruːz] Bluterguss
brush [brʌʃ] Pinsel
bulb [bʌlb] Glühbirne
bull [bʊl] *umg.* Blödsinn
bum [bʌm] *Schimpfwort* Penner
bump [bʌmp] *hier:* Pickel
butt [bʌt] *umg.* Hintern

C

capable ['keɪpəbl] fähig
carpet ['kɑːpɪt] Teppich
casual ['kæʒuəl] lässig
cause [kɔːz] Anlass; Grund
cavity ['kævəti]: (to) **drill a cavity**
  einen Zahn bohren
ceiling ['siːlɪŋ] Decke
chandelier [ˌʃændə'lɪə]
  Kronleuchter
charge [tʃɑːdʒ]: (to) **press charges**
  Anklage erheben
charm [tʃɑːm] Anhänger
  (Schmuck)

(to) **cheat** [tʃiːt] betrügen
cheek [tʃiːk] Wange
cheesy ['tʃiːzi] *umg.* abgedroschen
chin [tʃɪn] Kinn
cinnamon ['sɪnəmən] zimtfarben
(to) **chirp** [tʃɜːp] zwitschern
(to) **choke** [tʃəʊk] sich
  verschlucken
(to) **chuckle** ['tʃʌkl] kichern
(to) **claim** [kleɪm] abholen;
  behaupten
cleansing [klenzɪŋ] Reinigung
client base ['klaɪənt ˌbeɪs]
  Kundenstamm
coffin ['kɒfɪn] Sarg
(to) **commit** [kə'mɪt]: (to) **commit
  suicide** Selbstmord begehen
(to) **complain** [kəm'pleɪn] sich
  beschweren
concerned [kən'sɜːnd] besorgt
confidence [kɒnfɪdəns]
  Selbstvertrauen
confused [kən'fjuːzd] verwirrt
conscious ['kɒnʃəs] bei
  Bewusstsein
(to) **consider** [kən'sɪdə]: (to)
  consider sth. etw. für etw.
  halten; etw. in Betracht
  ziehen
considerable [kən'sɪdərəbl]
  beträchtlich
considerate [kən'sɪdərət]
  rücksichtsvoll
(to) **constitute** ['kɒnstɪtjuːt] etw.
  sein
convenient [kən'viːniənt]
  praktisch; bequem
(to) **convince** [kən'vɪns]
  überzeugen

court [kɔːt] Gericht
coward ['kaʊəd] Feigling
cranky ['kræŋki] übellaunig
crap [kræp] *vulgär* Scheiße
creep [kriːp] *umg.* unangenehme
Person
(to) **cringe** [krɪndʒ]
zusammenzucken
crush [krʌʃ]: (to) **have a crush on**
sb. *umg.* in jmdn. verknallt
sein
curly ['kɜːli] lockig
curtain ['kəːtn] Vorhang
curtain rod Vorhangstange
customer ['kʌstəmə] Kunde(-in)

D

(to) **dare** [deə] sich trauen
(to) **dare sb.** jmdn.
herausfordern
how dare you wie kannst du es
wagen
(to) **date** [deɪt] mit jmdm. gehen
(Beziehung)
date Verabredung; Begleitung
deaf [def] taub
defendant [dɪ'fendənt]
Angeklagte(r)
(to) **define** [dɪ'faɪn] festlegen
(to) **deliver** [dɪ'lɪvə] liefern
delusion [dɪ'luːʒn]
(Selbst)täuschung
(to) **deny** [dɪ'naɪ] bestreiten
dependable [dɪ'pendəbl]
verlässlich
(to) **deserve** [dɪ'zɜːv] verdienen
desperate ['despərət] verzweifelt
determined [dɪ'tɜːmɪnd]
entschlossen

devil ['devl] Teufel
diaper ['daɪəpə] Windel
dirt [dɜːt] *umg.* Klatsch
(to) **display** [dɪ'spleɪ] ausstellen;
zeigen
(to) **distract** [dɪ'strækt] ablenken
(to) **ditch** [dɪtʃ] sitzen/stehen
lassen
doll [dɒl] Puppe; *umg.* Schatz
doubt [daʊt] Zweifel
(to) **doubt sb.** jmdm. nicht
glauben
(to) **drag** [dræg] schleifen
dragon ['drægən] *Schimpfwort*
Drachen
drawer [drɔː] Schublade
(to) **drawl** [drɔːl] gedehnt
sprechen
drug [drʌg] Droge
dumb [dʌm] *umg.* blöd
(to) **dye** [daɪ] färben

E

(to) **ease** [iːz] behutsam bewegen
effort ['efət] Mühe; Aufwand
embarrassed [ɪm'bærəst] peinlich;
verlegen
(to) **embarrass sb.** jmdn. in
Verlegenheit bringen
(to) **employ** [ɪm'plɔɪ] beschäftigen
employee [ɪm'plɔɪiː]
Mitarbeiter(in)
(to) **encourage** [ɪn'kʌrɪdʒ]
unterstützen
engaged [ɪn'geɪdʒd] verlobt
entrance ['entrəns] Eingang
(to) **erase** [ɪ'reɪz] *hier:* ausgleichen
escalator ['eskəleɪtə] Rolltreppe
evidence ['evɪdəns] Anzeichen

evil ['iːvl] böse
(to) examine [ɪg'zæmɪn] prüfen
exception [ɪk'sepʃn] Ausnahme
(to) exchange [ɪks'tʃeɪndʒ]
   (aus)tauschen
exhausted [ɪg'zɔːstɪd] erschöpft
eyebrow ['aɪbraʊ] Augenbraue
eyelash ['aɪlæʃ] Wimper
eyelid ['aɪlɪd] Augenlid

F

fabulous ['fæbjələs] fabelhaft; toll
(to) face [feɪs]: (to) face sb. jmdm.
   gegenübertreten
fairy tale ['feəri teɪl] Märchen
faith [feɪθ] Vertrauen
fake [feɪk] unecht; gefälscht
fame [feɪm] Ruhm
familiar [fə'mɪlɪə] vertraut
favor ['feɪvər] Gefallen
fierce [fɪəs] *umg.* scharf;
   gutaussehend
(to) figure ['fɪgə] schätzen;
   denken
(to) fire ['faɪə] feuern *(entlassen)*
fist [fɪst] Faust
(to) fit [fɪt] passen
   (to) have a fit einen Anfall
   bekommen
(to) fix [fɪks]: (to) fix sth. etw. in
   Ordnung bringen
(to) flick [flɪk] schnell bewegen
(to) fling [flɪŋ] schwingen *(Haare)*
(to) flip [flɪp] wenden *(werfen)*
   flip *umg.* flapsig
(to) float [fləʊt] schweben
(to) focus ['fəʊkəs] jmdn.
   ansehen; sich auf etw.
   konzentrieren

fool [fuːl] Idiot
(to) forgive [fə'gɪv] vergeben
frame [freɪm] Rahmen
freaking ['friːkɪŋ] *umg.* Mist-
freebee ['friːbi] Werbegeschenk
frostbite ['frɒstbaɪt] *Sing.*
   Erfrierungen
furious ['fjʊərɪəs] wütend
fuzzy ['fʌzi] wuschelig

G

(to) gasp [gɑːsp] keuchen
gay [geɪ] schwul
(to) geek out [ˌgiːk'aʊt] *umg.*
   ausflippen
gift [gɪft] Geschenk
(to) giggle ['gɪgl] kichern
(to) glance [glɑːns] (kurz)
   schauen
(to) glare [gleə]: (to) glare at sb.
   jmdn. wütend anstarren
glimpse [glɪmps] Einblick
(to) goof [guːf]: (to) goof around
   umg. herumblödeln
gorgeous ['gɔːdʒəs] hinreißend
(to) graduate ['grædʒuət] die
   Abschlussprüfung bestehen
grateful ['greɪtfl] dankbar
(to) grin [grɪn] grinsen
grudge [grʌdʒ]: (to) hold a grudge
   nachtragend sein
guilty ['gɪlti] schuldig
gut [gʌt]: (to) have the guts *umg.*
   Mut haben

H

hallway ['hɔːlweɪ] Flur
halo ['heɪləʊ] Heiligenschein

handcuffs ['hændkʌfs]
Handschellen

(to) **handle** ['hændl] sich
kümmern

hawk [hɔːk] Falke

(to) **heal** [hiːl] heilen

heel [hiːl] Absatz *(Schuh)*

hedge [hedʒ] Hecke

hen [hen] Huhn

hesitation [ˌhezɪ'teɪʃn] Zögern

(to) **hire** [haɪə] einstellen

homeroom ['həʊmruːm] *Raum, in
dem zu Beginn des Tages die
Anwesenheit überprüft und
Informationen bekanntgegeben
werden*

honest ['ɒnɪst] ehrlich

horrible ['hɒrəbl] scheußlich

horrified ['hɒrɪfaɪd] schockiert

human ['hjuːmən]: **human
resources office**
Personalabteilung

humiliating [hjuː'mɪlieɪtɪŋ]
blamable; demütigend

humungous [hjuː'mʌŋgəs] enorm

I

(to) **ignore** [ɪg'nɔː] ignorieren

(to) **impress** [ɪm'pres]
beeindrucken

(to) **include** [ɪn'kluːd] einbeziehen

incredible [ɪn'kredəbl]
unglaublich

infatuated [ɪn'fætʃueɪtɪd]
verknallt

innocent ['ɪnəsnt] unschuldig

insane [ɪn'seɪn] verrückt,
wahnsinnig

(to) **insist** [ɪn'sɪst] darauf
bestehen; behaupten

insufferable [ɪn'sʌfrəbl]
unerträglich

(to) **interfere** [ˌɪntə'fɪə]
beeinträchtigen

(to) **itch** [ɪtʃ] jucken

invisible [ɪn'vɪzəbl] unsichtbar

involved [ɪn'vɒlvd] verwickelt

J

jail [dʒeɪl] Gefängnis

(to) **jeopardize** ['dʒepədaɪz]
gefährden

joy-filled ['dʒɔɪˌfɪld] voller Freude

judgement ['dʒʌdʒmənt]: **poor
judgement** mangelndes
Urteilsvermögen

justice ['dʒʌstɪs] Gerechtigkeit

K

(to) **kid** [kɪd] veralbern

L

lace [leɪs] Schnürsenkel

ladder ['lædə] Leiter

lap [læp] Schoß

layaway ['leɪəweɪ] *auf Anzahlung
Gekauftes*

leaflet ['liːflət] Prospekt

legal ['liːgl]: **legal matter**
Rechtsangelegenheit

liar ['laɪə] Lügner(in)

(to) **lie** [laɪ] lügen

(to) **lift** [lɪft] hochheben

linen ['lɪnɪn] (Bett- und
Tisch)wäsche

liquor ['lɪkə] Alkohol

(to) **lock** [lɒk] (ab)schließen

locksmith ['lɒksmɪθ] Schlosser(in)
lousy ['laʊzi] lausig
low [ləʊ] tief
(to) **lower** ['ləʊə] senken

M

made-up [meɪd'ʌp] erfunden;
geschminkt
major ['meɪdʒə] bedeutend
maniac ['meɪniæk] *umg.*
Verrückte(r)
marble ['mɑ:bl] Murmel
(to) **mention** ['menʃn] erwähnen
mesmerized ['mezməraɪzd]
hypnotisiert
mess [mes] *Sing.* Schwierigkeiten
(to) **mess sth. up** etw.
verpfuschen
(to) **mess with sb.** jmdn. zum
Narren halten
miracle ['mɪrəkl] Wunder
miserable ['mɪzrəbl] unglücklich
(to) **murder** ['mɜ:də] umbringen
mystery ['mɪstri] Rätsel

N

nail [neɪl] (Finger)nagel
nail salon Nagelstudio
necklace ['nekləs] Halskette
(to) **negotiate** [nɪ'gəʊʃieɪt]
verhandeln
nerve [nɜ:v] Mut
nerves Nervosität
(to) **get on sb.'s nerves** jmdm.
auf die Nerven gehen
nightmare ['naɪtmeə] Albtraum
nuts [nʌts] *umg.* verrückt

O

obnoxious [əb'nɒkʃəs] widerlich
obvious ['ɒbviəs] offensichtlich
occasion [ə'keɪʒn] Gelegenheit
odd [ɒd] seltsam
offense [ə'fens]: **no offense**
nimms mir nicht übel
offstage [ˌɒf'steɪdʒ] hinter der
Bühne
opportunity [ˌɒpə'tju:nəti]
Chance
(to) **oversee** [ˌəʊvə'si:] leiten
(to) **owe** [əʊ] etw. verdanken

P

(to) **pace** [peɪs]: (to) **pace yourself**
sich bremsen
pain [peɪn] Schmerz
(to) **be a pain** *umg.* jmdn.
nerven
pale [peɪl] blass
pathetic [pə'θetɪk] *abwertend*
jämmerlich
payment ['peɪmənt] Bezahlung
pecs [peks] Brustmuskeln
(to) **picture** ['pɪktʃə] sich etw.
vorstellen
pinstripe ['pɪnstraɪp]
Nadelstreifen
pitiful ['pɪtɪfl] mitleiderregend
(to) **plead** [pli:d] flehen
pointy-toed ['pɔɪntiˌtəʊd] an den
Zehen spitzzulaufend
polka dot ['pɒlkəˌdɒt] Tupfen
(Stoffmuster)
(to) **pose** [pəʊz] posieren
(to) **postpone** [pə'spəʊn]
verschieben
(to) **predict** [prɪ'dɪkt] vorhersagen

preoccupied [priˈɒkjupaɪd]
gedankenverloren
priest [priːst] Priester
pro [prəʊ] Profi
probation [prəˈbeɪʃn] Bewährung
protection [prəˈtekʃn] Schutz
(to) **prove** [pruːv] beweisen
psyched-out [ˌsaɪktˈaʊt] *umg.*
durchgedreht
public [ˈpʌblɪk] Öffentlichkeit
(to) **punch** [pʌntʃ] schlagen
puppy [ˈpʌpi] Welpe
purse [pɜːs] Handtasche

Q

(to) **quit** [kwɪt]: (to) **quit sth.** mit
etw. aufhören; kündigen

R

(to) **rave** [reɪv]: (to) **rave about
sth.** von etw. schwärmen
reassuring [ˌriːəˈʃʊərɪŋ]
beruhigend
(to) **recognize** [ˈrekəgnaɪz]
erkennen
register [ˈredʒɪstə] Kasse
(to) **refuse** [rɪˈfjuːz] sich weigern
(to) **reimburse** [ˌriːɪmˈbɜːs]
(rück)erstatten
relieved [rɪˈliːvd] erleichtert
(to) **remind** [rɪˈmaɪnd] erinnern
(to) **replace** [rɪˈpleɪs] ersetzen
(to) **require** [rɪˈkwaɪə] verlangen
(to) **resist** [rɪˈzɪst] widerstehen
résumé [ˈrezjuːmeɪ] Lebenslauf
(to) **reunite** [ˌriːjuːˈnaɪt]
wiedervereinigen
(to) **rid** [rɪd]: (to) **get rid off sth.**
etw. loswerden

ridiculous [rɪˈdɪkjələs] lächerlich
row [rəʊ]: **in a row** hintereinander
(to) **rub** [rʌb] auftragen
rude [ruːd] unhöflich
rumor [ˈruːmər] Gerücht
(to) **rush** [rʌʃ] stürmen
rusty [ˈrʌsti] rostig

S

sacrifice [ˈsækrɪfaɪs] Opfer
salary [ˈsæləri] Gehalt
salesperson [ˈseɪlzpɜːsn]
Verkäufer(in)
sane [seɪn] vernünftig
satisfaction [ˌsætɪsˈfækʃn]
Zufriedenheit
(to) **scratch** [skrætʃ] zerkratzen
(to) **screw** [skruː]: (to) **screw sth.
up** *umg.* etw. vermasseln
screw you *umg.* du kannst
mich mal
(to) **scrunch** [skrʌntʃ]: (to)
scrunch up your face das
Gesicht verziehen
(to) **scrunch your body up** sich
vor Kälte krümmen
secrecy [ˈsiːkrəsi]
Verschwiegenheit
selfish [ˈselfɪʃ] egoistisch
sense [sens] Ahnung; Sinn;
Verstand
serious [ˈsɪəriəs] ernst
(to) **serve** [sɜːv] bedienen
settled [ˈsetld] abgemacht
severe [sɪˈvɪə] schlimm
(to) **sew** [səʊ] nähen
shade [ʃeɪd] Farbton
(to) **share** [ʃeə] teilen
shaved [ʃeɪvd] rasiert

shift [ʃɪft] Schicht
shoot [ʃuːt] *Sing.* Aufnahmen
  (to) **shoot** aufnehmen
  (to) **shoot for sth.** nach etw.
  streben
shriek [ʃriːk] Kreischen
  (to) **shrug** [ʃrʌg] mit den Achseln
  zucken
signature ['sɪgnətʃə] Erkennungs-
skillet ['skɪlɪt] Pfanne
skin [skɪn] Haut
skinny ['skɪni] dünn
  (to) **skip** [skɪp] ausfallen lassen
sleeve [sliːv] Ärmel
  (to) **smash** [smæʃ] (ein)schlagen
smeary ['smɪəri] verschmiert
smirk [smɜːk] Grinsen
smooth [smuːð] glatt
smudged [smʌdʒd] verwischt
snarky ['snɑːki] abfällig
  (to) **snap** [snæp] *umg.* anfahren,
  anschnauzen
  (to) **sneer** [snɪə] höhnisch grinsen
  (to) **snicker** ['snɪkə] kichern
  (to) **sniff** [snɪf] schniefen
  (to) **snip** [snɪp] schnippisch etw.
  sagen
  (to) **snort** [snɔːt] schnauben
snotty ['snɒti] *umg.* pampig
  (to) **spill** [spɪl]: (to) **spill sth.** *umg.*
  etw. verraten
spirit ['spɪrɪt]: **good spirits** gute
  Geister
  (to) **spit** [spɪt] spucken
spooky ['spuːki] unheimlich
  (to) **squeal** [skwiːl] kreischen
  (to) **squeeze** [skwiːz] drücken
  (to) **stall** [stɔːl] zögern
  (to) **stammer** ['stæmə] stammeln

stapler ['steɪplə] Tacker
stock [stɒk] Ware
stove [stəʊv] Herd
stunned [stʌnd] sprachlos
stunning ['stʌnɪŋ] umwerfend
  (to) **stutter** ['stʌtə] stottern
subscription [səb'skrɪpʃn]
  Abonnement
  (to) **substitute** ['sʌbstɪtjuːt]
  ersetzen
subtle ['sʌtl] dezent
  (to) **sue** [suː]: (to) **sue sb.** jmdn.
  verklagen
sundae ['sʌndeɪ] Eisbecher
superpersistent [ˌsuːpəpə'sɪstənt]
  besonders hartnäckig
  (to) **supply** [sə'plaɪ] versorgen
  (to) **suppose** [sə'pəʊz] vermuten
    (to) **be supposed to do/be sth.**
  etw. tun/sein sollen
surgeon ['sɜːdʒən] Chirurg(in)
surgery ['sɜːdʒəri]: **plastic surgery**
  Schönheitsoperation
survey [sə'veɪ] Begutachtung
suspicious [sə'spɪʃəs] misstrauisch
  (to) **swallow** ['swɒləʊ] schlucken
swan [swɒn] Schwan
  (to) **swear** [sweə] schwören
  (to) **sweat** [swet] schwitzen
sweater ['swetə] Pullover
  (to) **swing** [swɪŋ] zum Schlag
  ausholen
swollen ['swəʊlən] geschwollen

T

tacky ['tæki] *umg.* geschmacklos
tan [tæn] braun *(Haut)*
  tanning center Sonnenstudio
taping ['teɪpɪŋ] Aufzeichnung

(to) **tease** [tiːz] necken
teeny ['tiːni] winzig
temperamental [ˌtemprə'mentl]
  launisch
tempted [temptɪd] versucht
theft [θeft] Diebstahl
thigh [θaɪ] Oberschenkel
(to) **threaten** ['θretn] (be)drohen
thrilled [θrɪld] begeistert
thug [θʌg] *umg.* Schlägertyp
thunderstorm ['θʌndəstɔːm]
  Gewitter
tight [taɪt] eng
(to) **tingle** ['tɪŋgl] zittern
toddler ['tɒdlə] Kleinkind
Tombs [tuːms] *umg. Bezeichnung*
  für ein Gefängnis in Manhattan
(to) **toss** [tɒs] schleudern
(to) **trace** [treɪs] zurückverfolgen
trash [træʃ] *umg.* Mistkerl
(to) **treat** [triːt] behandeln
(to) **trust** [trʌst] vertrauen
trustworthy ['trʌstwɜːði]
  vertrauenswürdig
(to) **tug** [tʌg] ziehen
turtle ['tɜːtl] Schildkröte
turtleneck ['tɜːtlnek] Rollkragen
tuxedo [tʌk'siːdəʊ] Smoking
(to) **twist** [twɪst] verdrehen

U

ugly ['ʌgli] hässlich
uncaring [ʌn'keərɪŋ] gefühllos
unconscious [ʌn'kɒnʃəs]
  bewusstlos

unlike [ˌʌn'laɪk] anders als
unsympathetic [ˌʌnˌsɪmpə'θetɪk]
  ohne Mitgefühl
upset [ʌp'set] aufgebracht

V

vain [veɪn] eitel
valuable ['væljuəbl] wertvoll
vending machine ['vendɪŋ məʃiːn]
  (Getränke)automat
violent ['vaɪələnt] gewalttätig
virgin ['vɜːdʒɪn] Jungfrau
vote [vəʊt] Stimme *(Wahl)*
vulnerable ['vʌlnərəbl] verletzlich

W

wallet ['wɒlɪt] Geldbörse
washcloth ['wɒʃklɒθ]
  Waschlappen
weak [wiːk] schwach
weapon ['wepən] Waffe
weave [wiːv] *eine Art*
  Haarverlängerung
weight [weɪt] Gewicht
whack [wæk] *umg.* (völlig)
  daneben
(to) **whine** [waɪn] jammern
witness ['wɪtnəs] Zeuge(-in)
  (to) **witness** miterleben

Y

(to) **yell** [jel] brüllen

X

X-ray ['eksreɪ] Röntgenbild

Chapter 1–4

1 What does Carlos promise Angie that he won't do when he gets the job at Macy's?

2 What do Carlos and Rosalia say about their father?

3 What does Carlos need to apply for the job at the FeatureFace counter?

Chapter 5–7

1 When is Carlos going to have his job interview?

2 What does Craig Denton think about Carlos's work?

3 What happens to Carlos at Eighth Street when he is on his way out of the subway?

Chapter 8–11

1 What does Gleason want to do with the photos he took for Carlos?

2 What does Lissette say about Valentino?

3 What happens to Rosalia?

Chapter 12–15

1 How does Carlos feel about Gleason?

2 What does Carlos suggest to help Shirlena Day with her skin problem?

3 What does Carlos ask Soraya?

Chapter 16–19

1 What is Gleason's reaction to the roses?

2 How do Carlos and his mom want to help Rosalia?

3 Where does Valentino want Carlos to go on the weekend, and why?

Chapter 20–22

1 What does Rosalia tell Carlos about Danny?

2 What does Shirlena Day ask Carlos to do to help her?

3 What does Rosalia tell Carlos and her mom about how she injured her face this time?

Chapter 23–27

1 What is Carlos's problem when he goes to the store on Sunday? What is he going to do?

2 What does Carlos do after Shirlena Day asked Christian to leave?

3 What is Valentino's reaction when he learns about Carlos's job at the studio?

Chapter 28–31

1 What do Carlos and Gleason talk about in the park?

2 What happens to Carlos and Gleason on their way out of the park?

3 How does Craig Denton see the situation about the makeup that Carlos took for Shirlena Day's show, and what is Valentino's opinion about it?

4 How does Carlos feel about his future?